A VIABLE
ALTERNATIVE

D. ANNE AUSTIN

 www.trafford.com
North America & international
toll-free: 1 888 232 4444 (USA & Canada)
fax: 812 355 4082

Contents

For Alice

In your light I learn how to love
In your beauty, how to make poems

Rumi

Introduction

Following my autobiography, "A Feather, Falling" this work seemed the natural sequel 1. A description of the way people, like me, seers, see and hear, smell and touch at a different vibrationary level in much the same way that an Alsatian dog has very keen senses and in both, it's a totally involuntary process.

These are all actual case studies. They all actually happened in different countries and I will describe the localities as well as the consultation.

One of the reasons that I feel this book will help people, is that the process has no political, religious or cultural borders. At first when asked to help a Chinese or Indian I would wonder if my being a Scot would interfere. Were our cultures and backgrounds too dissimilar to find a mid point? However we are chosen to serve for our suitability in much the same way that a computer has certain programmes. Each of us has gifts, experiences, friendships, familiar territories of our homes, holiday destinations, workmates, hobbies, favourite books and music and so on. Each of us, unique

In that programmed mass of knowledge, consciously and subconsciously, there is a vast field of data.

I found that working with different cultures I would be given the correct metaphor or analogy for the occasion and so the session would flow smoothly and intelligibly for both.

I wonder if this is the reason that I've taught in many cultures absorbing unconsciously the attitudes, preferences and life stories of my colleagues from S.E.Asia, India, China,

Japan. Which came first? The need for me to have this background or synchronicity or even accident!

Or would it have mattered, since I act as a channel for higher dimensions.

Chapter 1

A Unique Experience

It was a lush and beautiful approach of bamboo groves as I drove up to a magnificent home in Borneo, a large island two and a half hours flying time from Singapore. The gibbons were softly whooping from the nearby jungle and the harsh cries of birds announced my presence.

There was a red parrot walking up and down the table in the dining room where we had delicious coffee and cinnamon biscuits. Everything was chosen with artistry and love of beauty.

I looked at my hostess who had asked for my help. An exotically beautiful Indonesian-Singaporean artist who looked as if she had stepped straight out of Vogue magazine.

I felt shabby and dull in my teaching clothes which had to cover all of the body. The only time both of us could make didn't allow me to go home to change and shower.

1

So the session began.

There is a format that I follow having first said mentally,

'I work in light I work in truth I work in love, please protect us.'

This was taught me by an amazingly wise and gifted healer from London.

Session began.

First saw the ray to which she came into incarnation (there are seven,) violet. I knew from this that she was certainly a very creative woman who had the capacity to feel very deeply.

I began to feel uneasy for the darkness was all around her. Her material world was excellent. There was no trouble with finances. Her husband a respected professional man adored her. She was highly respected in her own field, traveling to Europe and the States where she held exhibitions. And yet........

The words came, though I tried to hold them back. She lived in daily fear for her life.

That she was in mortal danger. That someone from her past obsessed her every waking moment.

It was enough. Appalled I looked at her and said

'Please forgive me...don't know where that came from...'

She looked at me and took my hand.

'No one knows that I was married before, that I suffered most terribly as his wife and cannot bear children. I do not know if he is alive or dead but he threatened to find me wherever I ran. I live in daily fear.

We then narrowed the focus and help in understanding her situation followed and the seen knowledge that he was beyond the problems of this world.

This situation has stayed with me for all the years that have elapsed.

I never doubted from that moment the truth of what I saw or was shown. The unlikelihood of so elegant and charming a woman who could grace any salon anywhere in the world, being in close proximity to the criminal world was beyond my outer senses to comprehend. Never was there such a case of outer and inner truth so diametrically opposed.

Since that day I always trust the inner vision and ignore the outer façade.

Some clairvoyants choose to do regression therapy instead of addressing the problems of the present incarnation. I understand this, for empathizing and in many cases experiencing, the suffering that the person has gone through is very painful. Of course many problems and phobias arise from past life experiences so this approach is very healing. I believe we all can just alter the direction of the lens depending on the need of the individual, to past lives, present conflicts and clarifying future directions while emphasizing the power of the will and intention of the querent(the one who asks.)

If anyone begins to rely on guidance and not their own strength, they are asked not to return till they have put into place some of the suggestions for their healing. This may seem harsh but it is not loving to weaken others. The help given is to strengthen them to achieve more in life by giving signposts. Their will is paramount.

Chapter 2

Jack and Guinness

The room from which I was working was in the back of a New Age shop selling scented candles, incense, books cards and charms. The charm stopped at the curtain, for inside were packing cases, ornaments bought at job lots, a broom cupboard and me, behind another curtain. Usually with two sweaters on for it was pretty cold in the South West of England. I was still trying to blend some teaching with my spiritual work hence the different locations, some better, and some worse. Bottom line is, wherever people need help that is the place to be. And for me, being spiritual is being practical and grounded.

No point teaching meditation to some single mother who needs help to find a job to alleviate her financial stress, teach the meditation after she's in an improved situation!

So, voices sounded at the other side of the curtain and I was asked if a curious boy could come in to meet me.

That's how I met Jack and Guinness the dog, unsurprisingly, a black and white Border collie.

I disappointed him, I know, being so very ordinary when he was so obviously expecting satin .jewels and panache.

I knew he was too shy to ask me to perform for him.

But the words came.........'You are a very creative person who writes very well and with this gift of imagination you will succeed as a journalist before being well known as a writer. Follow your dreams and don't allow others' low expectations to influence you."

He blurted out, face scarlet, 'That is true...I write the best stories in the school!

Come on Guinness!'

Not bad to impress a cheeky ten year old! I wonder if Guinness was disappointed that I didn't look for him! That is so easy, for animals do not reject healing or seeing as people do, so conditioned are we to coming from the logical brain. Animals absorb and give out so easily, receiving and giving out healing.

I went on a horse whispering and healing weekend in Surrey which was a remarkable experience. The two youngest horses in the herd chose me to work on. They nudged me into a corner of the field and as we worked together the most wonderful trust emerged.

When the chestnut, Blessings .fell asleep against me, tears fell from my eyes.

In much the same style as Jack a young boy of around the same age came up to me at an exhibition in the West country. I think he snuck in under the guy ropes of the marquee.

He sidled up to me and whispered from the corner of his mouth,

'Are you the one who reads people's minds? 'I laughed and gave him a short explicit analysis of himself which satisfied him as he shot off, avoiding anyone in authority.

Chapter 3

Horse Talk

The best horse story happened in a market town in the South West of England. This area is a sacred area of Britain when Britain used to be called 'the Holy Island' to the ancients. Some of the most ancient monuments are there, the Tor in Glastonbury and Chalice Well, Stonehenge and Avebury, Wayland's Smithy where horses were magically shod if a coin was left, Windmill Hill, and all linked by the ancient pathway, the Ridgeway. This walk over moorland and hills takes between a fortnight and ten days to complete with many bed and breakfast places en route to make it easier for modern travelers.

It always amuses me to see on a board outside an old village inn, a sign saying, "Wild boar served today' We could be right back in the days of Henry the Eighth and velvet gowns and tournaments!

In a hotel overlooking the marketplace an old, very old, lady, came to see me.

As she sat down opposite me I saw several horses all shapes and colours behind and beside her. A beautiful chestnut with a white flash on his forehead was the closest. His head was over her shoulder, so lovingly protecting her.

I opened with the words

'Why so many horses all around you?'

They were as clear as the words on this page.

She smiled at me and said in an abrupt 'county' voice 'because I'm a horse breeder my dear.'

When I described the chestnut over her shoulder she knew immediately who he was.

'That was 'Blaze we were very close.'

So as the horses listened and were fully part of the session, from how many years back I have no idea, we progressed to her current situation.

She, in her late eighties, still rode daily also took part in carriage competition. She laughed as she told me of her many fractures but refused to stop riding no matter what her doctor advised.

What impressed me most about this great, spirited woman was that she was totally disinterested in herself or what would happen to her but totally focused on the reality of the well being of the remaining five horses in her herd..

One by one we looked at which would predecease her and what would be the best way forward for the ones who would go on living after her death. She was totally detached and absolutely determined to do the best she could for them in her absence.

I like to think that when her time comes she will be met by a herd of wildly happy, neighing horses, manes streaming in the wind as she springs on the back of Blaze, joyful in the knowledge that they never parted.

One of the most selfless people I ever met. She belongs in my book of stars!

Her helper phoned me some weeks later to say how much she'd enjoyed our session and how it had healed her of her anxiety over the remaining horses' future and later when she passed.

A privilege for me to meet her and her equine friends!

Chapter 4

Perth, Australia

The most isolated city in the world, Perth, Australia is a paradise of a place with green, rolling parks, vast beaches, even private dog beaches, and nearby, rose gardens, acres wide, with old and new varieties of roses and lavender. The Swan River makes for luxuriant green growth. Horses and riding stables and breweries complete this multifaceted city. Wild camels roaming free in the large desert to the east remind one of the very varied geography of Australia. But it is the birds that amaze and challenge the senses. It feels like a kingdom of birds and that they tolerate the presence of human beings. Flocks of brown ibises, and white birds which hang upside down from trees, their pink rimmed eyes looking decidedly ropey, as if they had a night on the town! Green parakeets and strange moaning magpies and crows create an orchestra of bizarre birdsong which is uniquely Australian.

Session

Every time I saw this highly intelligent business woman, I smelled ink. Eventually I said to her,

'I know it sounds strange but I keep smelling ink.'

'Not surprising,'she said, 'my late husband was a printer.'

So proof was given by the sense of smell in that instance. A keen gardener she designed, with higher help, an exquisite conservatory and many tiered patio for her exotic trailing plants.

Her great anxiety was for her grand daughter and an appointment was made.

Session

A beautiful girl came to see me, painfully thin, obviously anorexic and definitely hostile.

I didn't blame her a bit. Her mother and grandmother had insisted. Normally in those circumstances I would suggest that another solution could be found, but in this case, looking at the hopelessness in the girl's eyes I knew she was desperately in need of clarity.

She had nothing to live for she said. Her twin brother had died two years before from a drug overdose and her life ended on that day. A brilliant scholar she wanted nothing more to do with school, had no aspirations, just wanted to be with her twin.

Her brother, very handsome, full of fun came and stood by her right shoulder, arm casually draped over hers. He spoke of how he'd learned in the inner planes of different alternatives he could have chosen. (There is no blame attached at that level, pure love and understanding.) He gave his twin proof that it was him and her eyes filled with light and hope.

After he left, she was told that she was an old soul who had come back to work as a healer and that the suffering she'd undergone was the price to pay for the gifts of healing and understanding. When she heard the words:

'To study psychology from the basis of a twin who had first hand knowledge of the drug scene and of anorexia would be the most incredible route as a healer with first hand knowledge and compassion as lived experience.'

She cried with joy, her face radiant.

'I always wanted to study psychology,' she said,' but I lost my way.'

When it is a case like that where there is an instantaneous breakthrough of acceptance and understanding, it makes everything worthwhile.

Chapter 5

The Marine

It was a very hot day in Cyprus with temperatures of over forty degrees. I was driving to Limassol from Paphos to have lunch with a friend. The container truck in front of me stopped. I stopped. But the pick up truck behind drove straight into my little Subaru squashing me and the car into the container truck. The driver fled who had done the deed.

Miraculously, I was ok except for bruising and a back which is not quite as good as it was.

(The driver owned up to the police and took full responsibility later on in the day) My beloved little car was written off.

I was scheduled to be in Exeter and felt that as I was included in the programme for doing workshops that I should honour that commitment.

The room was packed and I began to talk about healing and healers and mentioned an American

Cherokee Indian, a former marine, living in Australia who always says,

'There is no competition among healers.'

At the end of the workshop, a handsome young guy came to see me. He was a marine and he told me that it was the mention of the American that had brought him to me.

His eyes filled with tears as he told me of his time in Iraq and how the carnage made him want to give up the military life to become a healer.

The words came.

'You are a healer but you can best serve your life's mission by retraining within the Army to become a psychiatrist to deal with the maimed men and women who return from war. Who better to understand them?

His face radiated joy and resolution as he said,

'It's the perfect solution.' And he hugged me so tightly.

In both of these case studies there was no seeming resolution of the problems. One, no will to live. The other overwhelmed by the pointlessness of war and death, longing for clean hands, I thought. An artist in a military body, usually the army generals of note fall into this category. Think of Lawrence of Arabia, Winston Churchill and so many others.

Chapter 6

The Gypsy

In Exeter again, in a different exhibition I came back after giving a talk, to find a shy man, dark blond curly hair and very vivid blue eyes waiting for me.

He was sitting so patiently and it touched me.

Session

During the course of this, I chose three relevant past lives to give him a better understanding of this incarnation. One of these was a musician who was dumb and could not speak.

He jumped to his feet in excitement and shouted,

'I am a musician with a lovely voice who is too shy to sing!"

When it was explained to him that he would pull his love to him through his singing, his confidence grew visibly.

This session made me very happy for this guy was a gypsy, a talented man who had the cage of his shyness opened from the understanding of where the block came from.

It was remarkable to witness the release. I learn so much from the great people I encounter. and often think how we worry about trivia and then we hear the problems of others which silence us.

Chapter 7

Phobias

When I refer to those who've died standing by a shoulder, it is not in the least spooky.

They oscillate at a very high speed of light as they come through the dimensions. I would be the first to run out of the room if it were a séance with ectoplasm! I have never attended a séance and the way I like best to work is always in daylight with lots of sunshine and oxygen around. Using nothing but my senses there is no barrier between me and the querent. Everyone works in a different way, not one better than another. My motto, reduce to simplicity, always.

Healing session

A friend with a phobia of tunnels asked for help using Neuro Linguistic Programming or NLP. She was put into a light hypnotic trance and fell deeply asleep.

I was a bit nonplussed for I needed to have indicators for' yes 'or 'no'

Carrying on with the session, ignoring the deep snoring, I asked for a yes response and up came her right hand! Checked the 'no' response and up came the left hand!

Fascinating how the mind can divide in that way while deeply asleep.

The tunnel phobia went, though it took her six months before she tested it!

Session

Same friend, another occasion.

Scanning her aura, she has health and weight issues, same tool, different application showed a problem with the thyroid gland.

She was adamant that it had been checked and there was nothing wrong.

Scanning ...this can be heard as a flat note over diseased tissue or seen as a dark patch where the rest is light. Most medical intuitives use both.

She agreed to go to a specialist and he found ten small abnormalities in the thyroid where ordinary testing had found nothing.

Many years ago, my then husband had a very bad rugby injury, a jackknife injury to the knee.

He swung the leg for six months, unable to bend it and I would scan it and say,

'There is nothing wrong with the knee.'

It became quite heated, for as a sports lecturer he had a much better knowledge of anatomy than I.

He was admitted to hospital and under general anesthesia the leg was bent. The surgeon told him that there was nothing wrong with his leg except that the muscles were so strong that they held the leg rigidly in place. Had he been a less fit man there would have been no problem!

Chapter 8

Missing Cats

Cats have always been a large part of our family life. Their characters so different.

Murphy, gentle, loving cucumber and mushrooms. Dylan, a fierce little cat who walked alone who loathed poor Murphy with a vengeance. Aphrodite who populated most of Scotland and northern England with her progeny! Domino who led dinner party guests into the house with tail held high. Merry, a fey little cat, with the tiniest miaow. Those were our Scottish cats who came with us, first to Germany, then on to Brunei.

As they lived into their early twenties, other cats joined the group. Noor who taught me the meaning of freedom. Mithras, prince of cats and Jason who tried his best to live up to Mithras' high standards. Core and Cadmus who take care of me in Cyprus who came from Saint Nicholas, Monastery of Cats.(Cadmus died bravely, killed by a snake in 2011)

Two Christmases ago I was contacted by four different owners of cats who were in desperate straits, their cats having gone away. One was in Australia. One in Cyprus. One in Sweden and the other in Greece.

Session

First cat in Australia. Saw her in long grass not far from the house casing the joint as it were.

Second cat in Cyprus. Saw her a long way away, having been startled by a passing car and got lost. Saw her crawling home after many days on her belly, paws cut and tender.

Third cat This cat had never been out of doors in its life. It lived in a third story flat in Stockholm and managed to slip out when his mistress shooed the other away from the door. A month went by and I would see this cat having a great time doing all the things he'd never been allowed to do. From a posh cat to a Thomas O'Malley cat! But I saw him being transported up stairs in a carrying basket.

Fourth cat In Athens having fun.

Conclusion all returned at different intervals. The first after ten days, hungry as a lion, sleeping for two days.

The second was hailed by the young guy who slept on the patio, watching for his cat to come back home was on military service. Took weeks to heal the paws.

The third was captured in a basket and taken up three flights to his golden cage.

The fourth looked worse for wear, but terribly happy.

The responsibility was huge. For all of us, animal lovers, we can imagine the suffering, gnawing away at us, day after day. The searching, looking out of the window, calling night after night.

As they called on a daily basis my relief was almost greater than theirs when they all got home. My direct link and what helped sustain me and the owners was the song that kept coming into my head when I looked for their wellbeing.

'gone fishin, instead of just a wishin.'

It's not all heavy stuff being on the spiritual path, there's a lot of humour too!

All help, gratis

Chapter 9

The Brahan Seer

A lady came to see me in Cyprus. She was attractive and needed help with her decisions regarding her love life.

An intelligent business woman, careful use of language was being used not to offend, yet still stick to the truth, as ever.

We were referring to her love when she said,

'We have never even held hands.....'

A long pause, and the words came.

'But I'm seeing you with him and it's more, a lot more than holding hands...'

She replied,

'Oh him? That's my lover, not the man I'm in love with.'

We both erupted with laughter.

Is there no privacy?!!!

This reminds me of the true story of the Brahan Seer who lived in the North of Scotland three hundred years ago. He was a seer of great repute in a country which is full of tales of the supernatural and most families have at least one fey person who interprets dreams portents and synchronicities. It goes with the misty mountains, isolation and rugged, amazing beauty.

He was called to the Countess who asked him what her husband the earl who was Fighting in France, was doing at that moment. He had to tell the truth, a prerequisite for seers.

'I see him in the arms of a French woman of the court, Your Grace.'

She was in such a fury that he was thrown into the dungeons there to wait for his hanging day

News went to the earl and he straight away jumped on his horse and rode without resting to stop the execution. Too late.

As he ascended the gallows the Brahan Seer took out his seeing stone, a pebble from the shores of a loch and threw it far and wide, saying

'The man who finds this stone will be from Strathpeffer and will have two navels and he will be my successor.'

That man actually does live at this time in Strathpeffer but whether he has the gift, I do not know.

History doesn't recount what happened to the countess for as the earl told her, the information was true.

An innocent man died for being true to his principles.

Chapter 10

Missing

In Sydney, Australia, that beautiful city with its heart, Darling Harbour I was taking part in an expo, three times the size of London's biggest.

Three of us, friends share an hotel room overlooking the city lights and we enjoy catching

Up twice a year with all that's happened. to us.

I am honoured to be allowed to participate with the dedicated mediums, healers and clairvoyants in Australia for the energy is very high and pure there, probably because the ratio of people per square miles is six in Australia to one hundred and fifteen in UK and the animals energy keeps the vibration high. Unfortunately too many people in close proximity cause pollution on every plane. It's rats in the cage syndrome, sadly.

On this particular day the organiser sent this lady to see me.

She had a resigned face and I felt her pain. Then I saw a young man at her shoulder, leaning his head against her with such affection. When I described him she said,

'It's my son!' and wept.

To be a clear channel the emotional plane has to be controlled by the spiritual or it causes distortion. Yet paradoxically, if one doesn't feel, there is no wisdom, only knowledge.

It was very difficult to hold back the emotion, for the young man, a student, worried unnecessarily about his exam results, jumped off Sydney Harbour bridge and his body was never recovered. No closure. As a mother of four I could not imagine the anguish.

As the mother was about to move away, her son called to me saying

'Tell her I'm riding the waves!'

As I spoke these words aloud, his mother's face turned to me with such joy.

'He loved to surf ...thank you, thank you.' And she left, healed at some level.

At another expo in London, I had the strangest request of my entire career.

The organizer was asked by a Russian lady with her Asian helper, if someone would listen to her question in Russian and reply in English.

I was intrigued and of course began to think what could be so dire a question that I was not to know the content.

I had not a clue how this would work, bypassing the conscious mind totally to bring from the ether a reply. There seemed to be a great deal of importance attached to it!

Session

Your name? Your father's name? For I was sure it related to the father.

Reading the names with my fingertips, I waited expectantly.

She went into a stream of fluent Russian for some minutes and waited, expectantly.

Half of me wanted to laugh my head off for it was so bizarre a situation. I had retrained

As a Teacher of English as a Foreign Language and had taught many lessons to classes containing Spanish head waiters, Swedish diplomats' wives, Italian models, Turkish students and Polish engineers. But this was the supreme challenge!

The other half of me began to speak confidently, explaining exactly where she would find the piece of paper she was looking for, not in the library but in the bedroom close to his bed in a book he was reading.

She was delighted, beaming at me.

'.Exactly the answer I needed, 'she said and shook my hand!

A fellow medium, a guy, with a black sense of humour said the question was probably,

'Where is mother?'

.When thinking about it afterwards I realized that all languages are simple vowels and syllables arranged differently. As I had read with my fingertips, not my eyes, why was it so odd that one would hear through the vibration and melody without the sensate cognitive aspect being necessary to the process, so I learned some more that day.

I guess she could've sung a nursery rhyme in Russian and with her intention being focused, still have gotten her reply. Intention is everything!

Chapter 11

Angry Young Man

I was in Newton Abbot and a young man pushed roughly past me to read my flier.

I was not happy.

When he threw himself down boorishly on the chair, he demanded I help him.

Now one of my sayings is,

'Love is an optional extra. Respect I will have!'

I told him to find someone else.

He became aggressive.

I told him that his attitude didn't impress me and I'd rather he left.

He apologized meekly and the session began.

Session

This man was very creative a musician, very good, but not quite star quality.

Tantalisingly near, poor guy, but not of the first order. In his frustration which made him rude and aggressive ….I felt so sad for his wife and baby daughter…..he was unbearable to be around.

He broke down, I think with relief that he was finally facing his reality. The dream that obsessed him was not going to happen But….there were two rivers flowing together, one was his music which he'd enjoy and create income from without the stress and the other was being a blacksmith working with wrought iron. His face went white as he whispered

'That was always my dream as a boy!

Public school background, parents were appalled.

And that's what he does, happy, creative, a loving father and husband. Angry young man, no more.

Chapter 12

Legal Matters

In USA a high achieving woman came to see me in the court system. At the level of her success she could not really afford to turn her back on the years she had spent in studying and defending important cases in the law courts.

Session

As I looked at her saw that across her back was a great deal of tension and the words came.

'I feel so many knives flying around you and that you live with this sensation daily.'

'Totally agree,' she said. 'That is my permanent state of being.'

The outcome of that particular session was the strategy for her to adopt in court, but also to become a judge where there would be no defending or prosecuting tension.

She was very happy with this counsel and has a much happier life now than before.

She had the target to aim for and the detachment to achieve it.

In Australia there is a very interesting lawyer who comes to see me regularly

And this makes me happy for I feel I understand his life, his aspirations, his joys and fears.

Session

Business matters examined and suitability of staffing. Relationship issues, his partner is charming and I feel an affinity with her.

But at the end, I always see a dog. This dog adores him and they are inseparable.

He laughs and shakes his head and says

'No time or place for a dog, but I had one I really loved maybe this is what you are seeing....'

At the end of a session, I have made cards, once photographs I had taken and had laminated with a word on the back now I use channeled cards from encaustic wax to signify human conditions such as farewell, joy, gain and so on. It always validates the session when the totally appropriate card is chosen by the querent.

In the case of this lawyer he chose, out of sixty four photographs. the picture of a friend's beautiful Samoyed!

We both felt the goosebumps rise.

Most psychics experience physiological sensations when something totally out of the blue occurs that we know is utterly true beyond a shadow of doubt. It's an excellent guide for it's entirely involuntary. Some feel the hairs on their arms stand straight up.

Others the hair on the back of the neck. Others temperature change. Skin pricking. Or goosebumps. Or someone's just walked over my grave.

I had a personal decision to make once that involved being patient not easy for me for I think and act quickly. As I asked this very spiritual woman's advice, the hairs stood up on my arm and simultaneously on hers. She said,

'Well we know the answer, don't we?'

Identical reaction, in total synchronicity.

Chapter 13

Crazy Earrings!

One of the more amusing aspects of this work is how very detailed the advice can be.

Sometimes I almost hesitate to give it for I think I must sound so very unintelligent.

Decide for yourselves!

In Cyprus I was approached by an elegant wealthy widow who naturally wished to know if she would ever have a loving companion.

Session

Having spoken about her business as a dentist and future business decisions, out of the blue the words came.

'You need to wear crazy earrings!'

We looked at each other and I shrugged.

A week later she phoned me, saying,

'You won't believe what happened! I was cleaning the teeth of this lovely man when he asked me out.

When we were having dinner I asked him why he had invited me out, he said,' I loved your zany earrings!'

I was amused and thought again, don't question!

The next episode of the earings was with a brilliant doctor in the States.

The same advice and the first day she wore them she made her love connection.

In Annapolis lady who had been on her own for years burst out as soon as she sat down,

'Remember I was told to wear unusual earrings, I met my guy the following day!'

Three cases, a hundred percent success rate!

It is not I, from the rational brain who selects what people need and interesting that only three people have been told that- it's not standard practice. There is no standard practice…every session is unique.

There was a great meeting in the south of England with an attractive athletic woman who made me laugh. She kept a friendly eye on me to make sure I remembered the times of my workshops and talks.

Session

Where she should live mainly. Proximity to children yet maintan her own life style as a healer. Her partner to be was approaching fast.

Because this is an issue that concerns many people, let's look at this in depth. When there is an issue of time involved the seer is working from the fourth and fifth dimensions or higher. Those dimensions are beyond time. Time doesn't exist there. Imagine being back in a Maths lesson…Heaven forbid….take the equation Length times breadth times depth and then add times time so $L \times B \times D \times T$

The ordinary rules as we know them in our dimension don't apply.

We see time as linear. It is not. That's an illusion.

Think of when you are at a gig and having a great time. Think of an equivalent time waiting to see the dentist. Both the same in linear time but how different in emotional time! Think of the phrases for shock…time stood still. We're knocked out of our ordinary perception of reality.

This isn't a cop out, by the way, for seers being wrong with time. They genuinely believe that the time frame they've been given, often, is right and yet they can be years wide of the mark, both ways.

Here is an instance of it working faster

Session

I was asked by a young woman when she'd conceive. She'd been married for five years.

She was told in her own time.

When I thought about it afterwards, I guessed about eighteen months from that time.

To me the phrase' in your own time' suggested that.

Actually she conceived that night, as she told me later.

So I have had many tapes done for me by excellent psychics, and all have been wrong with time. Everything else has been completely correct. The trend has been correct, wrong.time. Because we are impatient, it annoys us to be given inaccurate information, but actually the information is correct but from another plane where different laws exist.

In a sense, time bends.

So I approach time differently. I asked to be given a symbolic house, like a child's first drawing. That simple house would have a doorstep, a knocker, a garden path leading to the door and a garden gate. The kind of drawing a five year old has fun with.

Return to simplicity again!

If I see the beloved walking up the path, they are close. If they have their hand on the knocker, they will show up within hours or days. If they are outside the gate it will take a bit longer. I feel that if people know that the person is coming, it satisfies them, a little like knowing the parcel has gone astray but it's on its way!

It works for me.

Another symbol which I use a lot is about health issues.

When there has been a condition that is slowly improving, it will be shown as rings in the surface of water, expanding away from the epicentre..

Another is the dart board where the bull's eye is close and the outer rings more distant.

This book is just how I see things. Make up your own mind. If you feel someone you know gets it right time wise all the time, then I'll be delighted to be proved wrong!

Maybe the trees have it right, the concentric rings marking age. Concentric time or emotional time of dots is in the style of the Impressionists.

To return to my friend who looked out for my time keeping for workshops, she told me that on her way home, six peacocks preceded her down the lane. Two weeks later her beloved entered her life.

Very often when something life changing is happening or going to happen, some unusual sighting of birds, or animals precede the change.

A friend in USA told me very matter of factly that three toads had jumped over his feet, and that he'd not seen even one in twenty years. I told him to check up Chinese symbols..The three legged toad is terribly lucky. A pretty close fit!

My own close encounter while recently in Verona, New Jersey took place in a park. This creature I've never seen before was shuffling or ambling fast towards my feet in bare toed sandals, munching clover en route. Grey, quite big, flat ears, and fascinated by my toes! I wondered whether to stroke him then thought better of it, it being a wild animal of some sort.

A jogger ran by and I called over to her to ask if she knew what kind of animal was following me.

She said, 'I've never seen anything like this behaviour pattern. It's either a possum or a groundhog.'

It was a groundhog but this was in July so time will tell was it a random event or a notification?

This is a little like dream interpretations. It's one's interpretation and understanding that matters. Six people might give a different point of view, but the correct analysis will be felt in the gut, the true brain, not the cerebral brain.

Rational judgment is important here to make the distinction between really bizarrely different occurrences and thinking "It's a sign" on a daily basis. That way no one would take you seriously. Common sense is a good counter measure always. My rule of thumb is…. does it feel really exceptional? Check ten things it might be. If they don't fit, go back to your first premise. It was probably right all along. We must honour all our faculties.

Chapter 14

Shanghai

Shanghai is a fascinating, enormous city of over twenty five million inhabitants. As a nature lover I'm more at home with mountains, trees and water, but this city has an atmosphere. There are architectural styles of the nineteen twenties and thirties. Fashion trends still include the flapper style hats with flowers above the ear. Cyclists are everywhere, in droves. The bustle of the markets, the food stalls. It has Life!

Session

Japanese business man working in China, reversal of power roles. A lot of 'face' issues and cultural differences

Whether to return to Japan or take the new opportunity for working with the same firm in the US

USA definitely the best solution for it afforded an exit with dignity, so very important to the Japanese.

Also in Shanghai, I saw many diplomats.

Delighted that so many women held these important positions. One young woman, an advanced soul, who had sustained a terrible accident as a child and had both legs amputated and there she was, elegant and charming, climbing her ladder of success.

There was an amusing interlude with a young Japanese girl. She was beautiful as a pearl, a perfect example of traditional Japanese beauty.

Session

At the end of career, spiritual path queries etc the one that is always asked

'What will my mate be like?'

The reply, as always.'If you are told that he will be six feet four, blond and blue eyed, a Swede, what will you do if a gorgeous, five feet seven, dark haired and dark eyed Italian asks you out? Will you say I was told he would be …… and make a wrong choice. In other words, don't narrow the goal posts too much.'

There was a long pause as she looked at me a bit oddly, then said

'You have described my father exactly. He is a six feet four, blonde blue eyed Swede. I have taken after my Japanese mother totally.'

Another similar experience happened in Annapolis.

Session

'In your auric field you have the number eight energy which can manifest in ways such as winning two tickets to the Bahamas.'

'I won the tickets to the Bahamas and I leave on Thursday night, my partner's going too!'

We both laughed. It's serendipitous when this happens.

Here it might be good to look at where the information is coming from.

In the eastern tradition, they are called the Akashic Records That is my perception. That all that has happened in the world since before time is held in the ether. Actually modern technology is very similar to this way of thinking. Look at the storage capacity of a sim card or micro dot technology.

That explains the past and present but how about the future?

So imagine that Fate and Destiny mean different things.

God or Infinite love, intelligence, what you will, gave us free will so that we could choose to worship him.

Free will allows us to choose the path we walk. But suppose a destined meeting takes place and one partner is not free. Both recognize the significance of the other but have to wait till circumstances alter. The free will choice of the first is stymied by the impediments of the situation. Fate is what's holding the destined union from taking place, so rather like a road which diverges for a bit then returns to its original path, there is stalemate. Then Destiny steps in, overriding the individuals and their choices by bringing in the larger picture. Our free will hasn't been taken away but a higher overview has come into play.

If we look at time differently, then all things being known from the beginning of time, all our choices have been allowed for, with no interference of our free will but the conclusion is known outside of time.

My philosophy is;' Pull out the stops as if you believe you can achieve whatever you put your mind to, then submit to the will of the Universe.'

I always feel it's a bit wimpish to say,'Whatever......'

We co create our reality with our thoughts and actions. We bring into manifestation what we wish to be and therefore can cope with the disasters that arise in every life, for we've chosen them too, as our burning ground.

Chapter 15

Metamorphosis

In Cyprus some years ago a young Australian woman came to see me. She is a very animated and extravert character and sensitive within.

Session

Where am I going with my life? Marriage? Spiritual path? Art?

The words came

'Leave the marriage for you have no freedom and cannot live with this degree of control.

Another comes in who is fated and karmic who will protect and love you as you are.'

She returned to Australia, ended a deeply unhappy marriage which had made her into a shadow in the corner of any gathering.

She is now a vibrant, joyful woman fulfilled with the loving partner. Their love is palpable and gives me a deep sense of the rightness of light work.

So what is that?

My vision of it that we are in service to the world beyond our family responsibilities which have to be met first, before we can pursue our spiritual path.

Healers are working with light in our auras affecting all the planes of our being. The physical is the densest form of spirit in matter. The healing might prepare someone for the acceptance of death as a friend, not to be feared or it might be the reversal of the life threatening condition so that life continues. The healer doesn't choose which way it goes.

Seers are healers too. They drop seeds of light into the lives of people which grow into new ways of being, of living life more fully and satisfyingly, not necessarily following the path of wealth, but abundance in lived experience.

They can bring testimony to the bereaved, that life continues and it is by the endearing trivia that the best proof is given People often say,' But it's so banal what they say!'

Do they expect to hear the secrets of the universe issuing from the lips of the happy go lucky teenager who just drove too fast and was thinking of his girlfriend?

Some are called, usually couples, for maximum power and safety, to help those souls who are trapped in the material world, over to the next, and to clear houses and areas where the residue of cruelty and perversion remain like a heavy pall. Interesting that birds still don't sing where there were concentration camps.

To think in musical terms for a moment, the vibration or note to which we are called matches only those things which are compatible. So a medium can experience being a child who is a murder victim but never could lower the density to experience the thoughts and intention of the murderer. To do so would be to wound the vibration he/she came in at.

If someone decided with their free will to enter into the coarse degradation of such a being then they would have to have enormous physical and moral strength to return to their normal state. And what would be the point of allowing entities into the sacredness of the body? We are not circus freaks to be gaped at by the masses.

All of these healers are spreading light to enhance the planet by raising its vibration.

I had a vision once that is still with me.

Of an army of children, wearing brown tweed cloaks, carrying a candle within cupped hands.

A humble army, obscuring their bright colours under their plainness and uniformity.

There is a terrific saying by the theologian/philosopher, mystic Teilhard de Chardin

We are not human beings having a spiritual experience.

We are spiritual beings, having a human experience.

Chapter 16

Red Sox

There is a time in our lives where change is inevitable. Sometimes it's imposed and other times we choose it.

A very intelligent and gifted doctor came to see me. He had a high bureaucratic position in a hospital somewhere in the States.

Session

Scanning him healthwise, good, but high stress levels, inevitably.

He was given the advice to choose what he really wanted to do, that it was time he had the right to do what he wanted and not always what was expected of him.

He returned to the discipline which he loved and has created a very happy and fulfilling life without the stress. He appears years younger, travels and takes care of all his family members who are quite extraordinary.

When I scanned his health for the first time, he fell about laughing, saying,

'It took me six years of studying to know what you've just said! You can join the Red Sox!'

I think this even beat the admiration of Jack and Guinness! What a compliment!

I watch his life flower and think of the faith and wisdom that led this man from a life of power and wealth to a life which gives more satisfaction and where his great talents help so many people.

He created a new reality with the courage to start again.

It's the Geronimo factor, I think where you shout and jump, without a clue as to where you'll land!

A British man some years ago asked for help. His marriage was in ruins. His job, precarious and he was desperately worried about his children. No solution in sight.

Session

The business that you are in has a sister company in Dubai. A fresh scene would be excellent for you. The children will be best helped by a father who has a higher income and can help with their studies by being in a stronger position.

Clearing away the debris of the marriage will be healing all round. Fresh prospects will grow for everyone

Four years elapsed and I heard from him again to say, for my records, that everything he had been told worked out exactly as in the session. He had an excellent job with further promotion. He had amicable relations with his ex-wife. He had a new partner who made him very happy. His children had all graduated.

That is an example of letting go. When things begin to unravel in your life and there seems to be a recurring theme, we are often being given a nudge from the Universe to move on, let go, new horizons beckon. The more we resist the more we get of the same.

Clinging on to what has gone is pointless.

When we embrace the new challenges, we feel the current of life working with us. That's when we know we are in alignment with our Destiny.

Retrospectively, we see it, not when we're going through it.

If for example we are meant to emigrate with our family to a new country, the house we're in might develop some problems. At the same time, a new boss might come to our company and there is a personality conflict and what was a great job, now becomes a hateful environment where we're always on edge, at the mercy of a bully. Then the neighbours leave and a new set come in, who are nothing like the good friends who've left. The car breaks down repeatedly. This would be an example of the Universe knocking at your door, saying,

'Time's up…. just go!'

Once when teaching in Scotland I saw this demonstrated most clearly. A character clash between two educationists which was impossible to eliminate. Cat and dog. Oil and water. That's life though.

Eventually, it came to the senior going to the junior's desk and clearing away all of his personal things into a cardboard box.

How much better if the junior had accepted that his card was marked and moved with dignity.

Sometimes there is no alternative but to accept change as the best solution in very adverse circumstances. Better to accept a situation when the odds are too great against us and live to fight another day.

Chapter 17

Silent Onlooker

In this work often analogies are given to help people with psychological anxieties about their perception of themselves.

To take the flower kingdom for example. When clients are told that the differences between a sunflower and a daisy or violet are the same with the human condition, and that is just the way it is, they visibly relax.. Within a family group, where the worst battles take place, usually, some siblings are the violets, others the strong sunflower and there is no blame attached to being one or the other.

Similarly with the animal kingdom. How can a giraffe experience what it feels like to be a lion?

I see a lifting of oppression and guilt very often and the healing process begin. The outmoded family dynamics are turned on their head with a new viewpoint.

A psychologist came to see me in Greece. The wild wind swept area was a beautiful background for work, with the Aegean all around and the scent of wild thyme.

Session

She was a leader in her field and worked with very disadvantaged people and again, the exterior, elegant, beautifully dressed with imaginatively designed jewellery, did not match the picture that was forming.

Behind her stood her mother who hung back, saying nothing. Usually when the ones who have passed come through they are happy, smiling, back in the form where they were happiest. It might be they died in their eighties but come back in their thirties or twenties as a very pretty girl for example.

In this case I looked at the inscrutable face of the attractive woman who sat in front of me and sighed.

'I have to tell you that your mother will not speak nor look at you. She stands back just looking at her feet. I'm so sorry. Just can't understand this.'

The psychologist looked at me for the first time, as if she were really seeing me.

'Had you said anything else it would not have been the truth. As a child I had a terrible childhood with a schizophrenic mother who could have shocking rages if anyone as much as looked at her. A shopping expedition would be a nightmare for I was a very sensitive child.'

Again the pattern of the healer. Extreme suffering to bring forward the compassion from heart and mind to empathize with the pain of others and alleviate their suffering. I call it turning the pain inside out.

If we dwell on miserable things which occur in everyone's life from time to time, they eat away at us like an acid in the gut. If we lift our act to say,

'Ok, that wasn't fair but I'm letting go of it so it doesn't hold me back.' Then the pain is translated into something of value, where we can use the experience to add to our pool of wisdom for others in similar straits.

The resolution for this highly gifted woman was to bring forward her creativity which was untapped except for her choice of jewelry. She would write and become well known in that field., writing with humour in the face of adversity.

She has published a play, at her first attempt, which has been produced in London.

Chapter 18

Birth of an Artist

Kuala Lumpur is a city with an amazing mix of cultures, Chinese, Indian Malaysian and the indigenous mountain people. The architecture mirrors this, so that there's a fabulously ornate Hindu temple with a Chinese Buddhist one close by. Hindus believe Buddhism is the younger cousin of Hinduism!

The lady who came to visit me was very strong minded. A financier and coming strongly from the logical, cognitive side of the brain.

Session

'There is a strongly creative side here that is not being used.

You are an artist, quite simply.'

This was dismissed very vehemently, but still the words came.

'Deny it if you will, you were born to be an artist.'

Eventually she grinned and said,

'My parents are both artists and I am determined not to take that same route of poverty.'

'You are here today for you have reached stagnation in your life where nothing gives you joy, no matter how well paid you are.'

She reached for a tissue.

She gave up her work as a financier. Within six months she had her first exhibition which sold out. She does commissions and has created in a very short time a reputation as a very talented artist. I t just keeps on growing!

We met recently at the opening of a restaurant and she introduced me to her husband,

'As the one responsible for all of this.'

He replied,

'so it's your fault that the house is jammed full of canvases and there's no room for my golf clubs!'

Chapter 19

Playwright

One of my favourite uses for this gift is in the field of literature.

In Cyprus there are wonderful outdoor theatres or amphitheatres, built of stone, circular or semi circular, usually with the sparkling Mediterranean in front, and the arc of the star filled sky above. Since there isn't light pollution the stars are very clear and especially in August and November there are many meteors and shooting stars.

It is a perfect place for Greek drama or Shakespearean plays. I saw a breathtaking Midsummer. Night's Dream against this background in Curium.

A quick moving, vital woman, actress, producer, director consults before a new production and I absolutely love it!

Session

'These are the plays…which do you think would fit into the year's programme best?'

The leading actors are male in the main and here are some of the names.'

We then hone in on the strengths of the performers and their suitability for the role.

We then look at the set, the lighting and music.

The whole thing is fascinating. It simply means turning the lens very specifically to a given scenario.

The plays have been very well received and again this woman has an enhanced life for she is being herself and stretching to bring out her gifts and love of the theatre on a small island. That makes for happiness!

I wonder if there could be a new job specification somewhere as a metaphysical director!

It was in Sydney that I met a gifted medium who taught me encaustic wax technique for art and also for doing life soul path art. He told me to take it out round the world and I've done so, doing workshops and talks and teaching the technique.

I see it as an important part of my healing/seeing work for it is a way in to the higher planes and it interacts with the medium so that the pictures form by direct intervention.

This is the process

The querent chooses five colours from a wide selection of wax tablets. They are jewel bright colours.

The medium has a small iron which looks like a traveling iron but has higher calibrations which is heated and ready.

When the five waxes have been chosen they are applied by the medium in the sequence they were chosen in horizontal stripes. It doesn't matter if they drip one on to another for they will mix in the process.

The iron is moved in one direction only from the bottom of the card to the top twice without going back over the applied wax.

Card is waxed A6 size.

As the medium puts the iron to the card, he/she says the words,

'This is the life soul path of (, let's say,)

John Smith

The pictures form and then the card is left to dry.

Finally, when dry, it is polished lightly with a tissue, stroking away, not rubbing up and down.

It is good to keep it clean and unscratched inside a cellophane envelope.

Then a short hand written analysis is given.

These are amazingly accurate in the detail.

I was in Greece and I was doing a session with wax with a creative teacher of dance.

Session

Looking at the bottom inch which signifies the first twenty years or so of life there was a tiny perfectly executed ship, incredibly detailed. Pointing ti it, I said the words.

'At eighteen there was a very important sea voyage which changed your life.'

She screamed out loud and I was shocked at her reaction.

'That's when I left South Africa for Britain.'

Maybe she just thought it was an interesting game till that point, I don't really know.

So using words and using pictures with the addition of spiritual intelligences from a higher plane of development, elucidates the sometimes hopeless situations we may find ourselves in.

It is in the letting go of the conscious mind that the deeper awareness of ourselves and our life's purpose can emerge.

The very first life soul path work I did was for a boy in USA

He was then eleven years old and I had a dilemma. A child's problem is usually addressed to some extent in the session with the parent. Most seers wait till a child is sixteen before they do a private session, to give them respect. My way round this is to suggest they have a life soul path session. I told M. that I'd send him his life soul path from Cyprus and asked him which colours he'd choose.

Five years later I can still see it in beautiful shades of blue white and red, mainly. A waterfall and behind the waterfall another life of joy, success and absolute happiness.

For whatever reason all the water in the forefront signified a deeply emotional early start followed by calm and success. It is still by his bed and still gives him the will to look beyond.

These are interactive. I notice that when I use my own symbolic cards from this process to validate the spoken session, people linger over them and are affected deeply by the meaning of their own selection.

They are without form yet touch the emotions powerfully.

They remind me of eastern art which is empty enough for us to fill in the spaces.

Often lotuses form if the person has had many lifetimes in Egypt. Mountains suggest high endeavour.

Three of us in Sydney had ours done at the same time.

A's was all violet, though she had chosen five colours, only violet came out on the white card. In the centre was a cave and within the cave a Buddha like figure in the lotus position.

H's was all green, and all trunks of trees.

Mine was in three sections. Down the left hand side flames and fire, like a dragon. The middle section was violet, a violet woman stood in a violet flame. The third portion was green. A monk like figure dressed in green carried a sword.

A has very good gifts one of the leading mediums of Australia. She is also an archaeologist and anthropologist.

H is a horticulturalist as well as a medium.

And there's me.

We all agreed they were totally right as we saw ourselves.

Once when in Shanghai I did a number of these life soul paths for therapists and of course they all compared notes.

(Only one can be done in a life time for obvious reasons)

One therapist came late and she is a person I like a lot. She is a very gifted interpreter.

True to form she wanted six colours, so I duly obliged.

When she got it she then worried that she hadn't chosen correctly and asked if I'd do another with five colours only.

I was interested to see the comparison myself.

Almost identical in every way, so it's not random at all! As she, a doubting Thomas, had expected.

Two years ago I made my first set of cards I loved the one for joy which reminded me of a little boy, hair standing on end, shooting through the planes. Yellow predominantly.

A few months ago I made a symbolic set and the same image for joy emerged. Without my doing anything or even thinking of the previous card.

A friend in Cyprus, an animal lover, who was mainly responsible with her husband for the removal of twin bears from the zoo who had been in captivity for fourteen years, asked me to produce her life soul path. Five colours were applied and again only one colour came out. Green and everywhere, bears. On rocks, in water, bears everywhere.

Two pictures jump to mind as I sit here typing in very high temperatures with fans on either side of me.

One..This is the one for my daughter, who is an artist,

It was like a beautifully executed picture of a Pierrot clown doing a handstand on green grass with a sky, so blue, above. Every feature of the face finely drawn. Red cap on head

The second for a brilliant astrologer in England who writes books and is a lecturer.

I told him I'd make him one and he duly chose his colours.

The result looked as if you were looking down on the surface of planets from above; You were in space looking down. It was spellbinding.

He phoned me, not his usual cool self and said,

'I never expected anything like this. It's incredible.'

And so it was, .as is his life.

Animals are very much a feature of this art. Wolves come through, dragons, fish, birds, dogs, cats horses and so on.

They seem to have a life of their own and grow almost before one's eyes

Chapter 20

Mutual Healing

I decided to do the art work myself for this book so spent time choosing cards which used colour and would give out energy to the reader if they meditated on the one they were drawn to.They are interactive.

There's humour up there, or out there, or in there, whichever dimension we wish to use!

Best if the reader decides for himself which means most to him, and why.!

One of the most important uses of the gifts I was born with was working with a wonderful woman in Brunei who had motor neuron disease.

A doctor I was friendly with asked me to go and visit to see if she would be prepared to see me. His thinking was that as a seer, (he knew that without my saying, for he was a healer too.)I could use my gifts to interpret what she felt. She had already refused to see the American therapist who was a very nice woman, so I wasn't sure what would happen.

The house was grand and her bedroom had every amenity, hoist and medical aid to help her cope with this condition which had left her with only the ability to blink once for 'yes' and twice for ' no.

She had warm brown eyes, a widow's peak and long dark hair. A very pretty woman of forty two with two sons. She had been bed bound for four years and she had turned away from everyone, neighbours, friends, even the doctor for a year. Her husband and the domestic staff were the only ones she met.

That day when the doctor and I went to meet her, we had a minor argument about something trivial but I was holding my ground. She was looking at me and although her face couldn't smile, it was there in her eyes. When doctor asked her if she wanted me to come she blinked,' yes..'

So our visits began. Truthfully she gave me a lot of healing by just being there so tranquilly for my life was teaching, studying Ayurveda and doing welfare work as head of a committee to further the life of teachers there.

I wasn't sure what to do, so reckoned a bit of massage with oils, touch is always important on the hands and feet, reading an excellent book," The Wind in the Willows 'and most importantly, putting my hands an her head to find out what she was feeling and thinking, always with her permission first.

She was a science graduate.. Her mind was totally alert. She would be anxious about her son at university in England. I would always check if I got it right. When she was angry I could feel it and when the frustration was intolerable, I would speak the words and see the relief in her eyes.

It was a loving friendship that grew. I would tell her the things that made me mad at school. She liked to know what went on in my life. Sometimes I'd look longingly at the other bed in the room and say,'I could sleep for a month.'

Because the school week was split into Monday to Thursday, Friday off as the holy day in an Islamic country, Saturday back to school and Sunday off, the fatigue would grow.

Once I was invited to a child's party at six and her mother's straight after. I packed the gifts, laid them with the cards on the dining room table, ran a bath, putting bubble bath in and lay down for a few minutes till the water cooled at three pm.

I wakened at 10am the next morning, nineteen hours of uninterrupted sleep. Sadly, there was a drowned gecko floating among the remains of the bubbles.

These visits continued till one day I told her I'd bring her a violet plant from Miri a town in Sarawak and that I'd see her the day after getting back.

In the market place, having bought the flowers, I saw a black tortoise with a yellow stripe under its eye. My friend told me it would be eaten, so I bought it on the spot and lettuce and bananas for it to eat, Such powerful front legs. I sat with it in a plastic bag all the way home. The only place for it was the bath till I could think of a better solution.

I gave him the name Achilles for he looked like a general with his stripes.

I went out to the veranda to put the violets there for the next day and there was L. smiling at me and standing. I said, 'L?'

The phone rang. It was doctor to say that just that moment she had died.

The funeral was the next day as is the custom. All that day she was with me in the car, stretching, laughing, talking to me all about her tennis championships, her mother also being a championship player. I had to tell her to settle down for I was driving, but she was so elated that she could move and be herself again. She knew of course that I'd bought her violets for she saw them on the patio.

When I met her mother I told her of the tennis and all that L had chatted on about. She nodded to everything.

Her son aged eleven was with his grandmother and I told them about Achilles. They spoke of the family's love of these creatures, of Sam in England who was always escaping and being brought back by children who knew him.

I heard L's voice clearly in my ear.

'Go home and bring him here.'

So I did, with the lettuce and bananas, and driving with one hand.

It gave the brothers a focus on building a home.

Some time later at the airport, I met the boy again.

He ran after me to say

'It wasn't a tortoise, it was a turtle and we still have him.'

After the day of the funeral I never saw her again, but I think of her often and her amazing courage.

That was one of the best uses of the gifts I was born with and a doctor with imagination got me to use them.

Chapter 21

Bournemouth

It was a dismal day in Bournemouth and I shivered at the bus stop on the way to the spiritual healer's sanctuary.

I had been tested to see if there was healing in my hands and if my intentions as a Buddhist would entitle me to join the others. It was explained that being a Buddhist I would not be able to be a church medium or healer. This was fine with me for I had no intention of affiliating with any religion, thinking that healing was like sunlight or oxygen, there for us in the natural scheme of things.

They were lovely people to work with, very dedicated and unselfish and those who came to be healed were very appreciative. They said they felt the warmth and healing flowing and this made me happy.

In Bournemouth too I made many good connections with healers and psychics from all over Britain when they come together once a year and a lot of good work was done as well as sharing experiences and cases, anonymously of course.

One such had bought a beautiful very old property in the south of England. She and her husband, artists, did a lot to restore the property, alas without crucial planning permission.

Session

What is the best way for us to tackle the local council?

Can we ask for planning permission retrospectively?

The name of the officer is/ should we deal with A or B/

It was a difficult case for the law is very firm about protecting old properties.

A compromise was reached and it was less of a nightmare though prolonged than had originally been dreaded.

The amusing thing for me was that I was on my way to Heathrow and China the following year and when she arrived at the place, I had gone. So we did a session on the phone at Heathrow with very curious glances directed at me with my recorder in my hand. They must've thought me a journalist!

I've described the return of the cats and now the return of the jewellery!

In England an elderly lady was very upset for her engagement and wedding rings had gone missing.

Session

'I see this lady in her dressing gown and she is sitting in a winged armchair. She's reading. She's quite a heavy lady and she's wriggling round to be more comfortable.

Look right at the very back of the left hand side of the chair, You will find them and she will be happy.'

Two hours later the phone call came.

'We've got them exactly where you saw them, right at the very back and deeply within the chair.'

Soon afterwards I was in USA and it was an eternity ring that had disappeared.

Session

'It has not left the house It is hanging somewhere where you wouldn't expect to see it.

Look up, not down'

It had caught a hanger as a cardigan had been removed.

Joy at its return.

The loss of possessions with sentimental value is painful, but sometimes rings go or just mysteriously disappear. Sometimes the owner just doesn't need it anymore and the mineral goes to someone with a need. Very often amethysts do this. They are very spiritually evolved stones.

I have a pendant which is very special to me. I thought the provenance was amazing.

The young guy who made it was a boat builder, yachts and so on He thought he'd try silversmithing and taught himself.

He found a huge chunk of fluorite and taught himself how to facet it into a semi precious gem stone.

I thought it was incredible that this beautiful piece of jewellery could come from a boat builder. I loved the connotation of a master craftsman moving with such ease between disciplines! He works from Glastonbury.

At this time I was also healing as well as seeing. I had studied Yoga to teach,

Ayurveda, Crystal healing, N.L.P. Aromatherapy, Advanced crystal healing, Indian head massage, and had become a Reiki Master.

And lately, Flower essence healing in USA

So the desire to heal is strong and in all the seeing there is a strong element of healing the whole life too.

I reckon we're multi faceted and do what is required of us when the situation is correct.

Like the boatbuilder cum silversmith!

Chapter 22

Financial Adjustments

In Britain and America two case studies were very similar Each involved money shortages where legal situations and lawyers said 'There is no insurance here.'

Session

'Go through papers very carefully doesn't matter how often you have done this. There is an insurance claim to which you are entitled.'

Very reluctantly for these are two highly intelligent people, they followed the advice to their advantage.

The second in the States involved a young widow who was suffering a lot financially as well as the grief at the tragic loss of her husband.

Session

'Get a different lawyer to deal with your case. You should be receiving a much higher pension than has been awarded.'

When I saw her recently she gave me a huge hug for the successful outcome.

In both of these cases neither had an inkling of their entitlements and intelligent people, both. I find this very interesting for Mathematical stuff is anathema to me. So that didn't come from my mentality.

Usually the sessions I do are with healers or people wanting to know life direction, what discipline to follow but these were very specific about their rights, even though neither knew they were being short changed!

It's a little like radar that goes straight to its objective without the knowledge of the seer.

Chapter 23

The Little People

I was in London- a very attractive dark, curly –haired young woman came to see me.

She was so jolly, I found myself laughing with her over something she said.

Session

'You have a very unusual job which you love. It seems totally incongruous for a person of your looks and age.'

'I am an embalmer with my own business.'

There is a man standing at you right shoulder who loves you very much and is thanking you for doing such a good job with him. He loved his send off, you did a great job.'

He's laughing and pointing to his left foot and saying you will know why.'

By now she's laughing even more merrily.

I couldn't straighten out that foot and it really annoyed me!'

Her favourite colour was red. She was one of the most fun loving people I've ever me, loving to dance, go out clubbing with her mates and her little daughter had a fabulous name!

She got the proof she needed that her uncle was alive in a different way and well and I learned a lot about not stereotyping people!

In Sydney a guy came to see me. Straight off I was seeing texts, words and sentences all floating around him.

Session

'You are a writer I believe and I think this writing has to do with your Irish heritage, for there are several leprechauns leaping about all around your knees!'

He was amazed and delighted for he was writing about these very beings and they made themselves manifest to encourage him!

The session went on and they remained till the end. In this time he was given publishing advice.

I was in Somerset and these two people came to see me. I have a lot of respect for them for they are in the forefront of environmental advance in the south west of England. She left her job on the strength of a session and she has grown, so fast, so quickly.

Her husband is covered in tattoos, was a biker and has the best healing gifts and is a seer.

He has the ability to see and talk to the Little People or Fairy Folk and they were trying to work out which plot of land- there were three to choose from

Session

It's not number one, that's too dear.

It doesn't matter if it's number two or three for you will buy both in time.

Then you plant in the microcosm for the macrocosm and you will teach others'

I asked as they were leaving,' Have you seen the little folk recently?'

He replied with a smile.

'I heard them talking and saw them and said, 'shouldn't you be a bit quieter?'

'Can you see us? 'they replied..

'What should we do with this piece of land?' he asked.

'Something nice' and they disappeared.

Chapter 24

Greek Tragedy

Cyprus is one of the most beautiful places in the world. Ancient, rugged and with the most wonderful light.

A Cypriot lady came to see me with her daughter aged eighteen as translator. I was teaching with the British Army at that time as well as doing my healing work. This involved getting up daily at 5.25 am, the same time I had to rise in Brunei to get to school on time. In both places the school day began at 7am because of the heat.

She looked very sad and withdrawn. Her energy was very low and I felt a great wave of sympathy sweep over me.

Session

Archangel Michael standing behind her, sword drawn.

Straight away the words came,

'What you suspect is entirely true. You are a most wronged woman.'

The daughter gasped and began to cry. She went over to her mother, flung herself down on her knees and began to cry.

The mother's face had changed in the meantime. Something like pride struggling through and honour satisfied. We exchanged glances, woman to woman, total understanding.

Having given her daughter time to compose herself and water to both, the words continued.

'In your family there is dissention and you are being made a victim. They are saying you are menopausal, mad, to believe such wicked things, but they are true.'

In a quiet voice, in Greek, the mother began to speak.

'For ten years my husband has been having an affair with my brother's wife. I know this is true, but the whole family shout at me and call me names No one believes me but you, and now my daughter..

This was Greek tragedy in the twenty first century.

This woman's spirit had almost broken in the face of the family's desire to push unpalatable truth under the carpet for the sake of the family's name, standing in the community and protection of property, for dowries would be involved. And of course a woman in a male dominated society? Who would take her word?

Light was returning to her eyes. She looked younger, not happy, but free.

Advice given. 'You will not change this situation between the two, but you can change your life. Insist that he provides you with your own place with dignity, or stay with the situation for your economic and social standing, but have nothing to do with this man.

He can not harm you any more for you know this is the truth. Have no more doubts about your own sanity. You are a very brave woman.'

I still believe this is one of the worst cases ever.. Not the affair, that happens, but the systematic dismantling of a woman's mind and other women would have been party to this. It beggars belief.

Karma would settle this. Her pain would be avenged, not by her or any human agency but by the immutable laws of the Universe.

Like me, she had a strong devotion to Archangel Michael, the guardian of truth.

Chapter 25

Cyprus Encounters

A s shown in the last chapter, the family is extremely important here in Cyprus which has many benefits in some way, not in others. Help is given to young couples so they get a very good start in married life. The father builds each of his daughters a house so there is no mortgage when she marries. By the time the young couple's own daughters grow up the father is in a stronger financial position to build. It's a very logical and pragmatic method of doing things and also the daughter has the protection of her father and brothers in the event of her husband misbehaving!

But Heaven help the guy who reneges on an engagement.......Melbourne, Australia isn't far enough away to avoid retribution! There are many Cypriots who live and work there in daily connection with family still in Cyprus.

The priest, .this is the Greek Orthodox faith, blesses the engagement, the young couple move in together with the blessing of both families and they usually marry when the first child is on the way.

I have been at many weddings where the radiant bride in white, trailing lace and white roses in her hair has come over to me and said proudly, patting her stomach,

'Six months pregnant, isn't it wonderful?'

Different countries, different customs.

It makes me smile, no sham, no shame, for the priest has given his blessing! All is well!

A very good man comes to see me. He is in the government and by profession an architect. It was a struggle for him, with his conscience, to see a non Greek and non Greek Orthodox seer. Or perhaps a seer of any kind. He is deeply religious and one of the best people I've met here.

I saw the Blessed Virgin Mary close to him and that is very rare. Usually it means that when a child lost a parent, she would appear in her young guise before becoming a mother.

That was the case here. He was left as the only son and his father died when he was three.

So he took care of his mother.

Session

'You have a great deal of responsibility and while it is good to be dutiful you have taken it to the extreme level. Duty is emblazoned on your forehead!'

He laughed and nodded his agreement.

'You wanted to be an artist but chose the profession of architecture for the stability of the family. You are a creative man who lives his life from the path of duty. You love music and love to sing.'

Tears filled his eyes.

Begin to paint. Have your own exhibitions, they will be successful.'

A much freer man now who honours who he truly is.

I was asked to meet a man at a venue in Limassol.

He had lost his daughter, very tragically when she was holidaying in America.

When he came, he did not come alone as I had expected, but with his wife and two sons.

It began. I explained that I would only speak to the father for there were four of their auras and only one of me. The wife understandably, who was heart broken kept interjecting, and I explained it hurt my body when she did this.

I think in her grief that didn't really matter.

Session

Her daughter came through, standing by her father, full of light, laughter and joy.

She gave many messages that only she and they could have known. She gave respect to the older brother who is a healer, and ruffled the hair of the younger brother and teased him. She explained how she had done what she had come back for in life and had to go

. She told them she would never leave them.

It was harrowing to feel their grief.

The father said, 'But she had no children, how could she say she'd fulfilled her life?

At the end he was overcome as they all were with the proof of her continued existence.

And they wanted to make an immediate next appointment.

I explained that I had used the power of mediumship to give them proof, but to leave it now and live their lives most fully for her too. This is a healthier way of dealing with loss

Once, ok

In our conversation the father asked if she would come back in another incarnation but said so sadly,

'But not in the same form'

'What was it you loved, her body or her soul? was the reply

Chapter 26

Justice

Dublin is a wonderful city with its bookshops, elegant buildings, wide streets and history.

I love strolling round, looking at the soft colourful woollens, lace goods and fine china.

At an exhibition there two sisters came to consult, or rather, a sister and a sister in law.

They were both in their thirties.

They were very direct in their enquiry. They didn't want an' unfocused session but 'an extremely focused one ' similar to the Russian lady in London.

Session

'There is a man here and he is very anxious about his family and the distribution of his property.'

'That's my dad,'said the dark haired sister.

'That's my father in law, 'said the other.

'There's a brother involved here as well, isn't there?' the words came.

'Well, yes,'said the sister in law

The dark haired one lent forward

'You see the problem is that my dad died recently and then my brother, three weeks after, so the will is no longer relevant.

The sister in law said

'So I think the estate should be split between the two of us.'

The dark haired one said,

'I want to know what dad wants us to do.'

In came the father and the brother who said, 'My daughter has to be safe.'

I asked how old she was. Eleven years old.

There was a house and a business that the father and son had built up together.

In his will the father had left the house to be split three ways and the business to go to his son

I asked the father what he wanted.

He almost shouted, such was his vehemence,

'Let the will stand! Let the will stand!

And the dark haired sister stood up, said

'Thank you dad, I'll do what you say.'

And the little girl's inheritance was safe.

Direct intervention and an aunt with integrity.

Chapter 27

Slowly does it!

People from all professional backgrounds often say,

'I want to give up my life as a lawyer and become a healer,' for example.

The advice invariably given is to splice together the law practice and the healing simultaneously, not to cause great tsunamis of reaction in their lives but to progress slowly.

I know those who have given everything up and two years later they are bankrupt and bitter.

Being spiritual doesn't mean giving up common sense!

Many religions, including Islam and Buddhism, state clearly that we must fulfill our family obligations fully before going off on our spiritual path.

When a client base has been established then job sharing can be an option or doing three days a week in the law practice, the rest healing

Chapter 28

Schtumm!

The worst kind of situation is when someone comes for a session and totally avoids eye contact and is not going to any indication of the accuracy of what you say.

They build a barrier by their own behaviour and it sours for me the session, even though they say at the end,

'You were totally correct all the way through and I feel great."

Why behave with so little grace?

A fabulous example of this was told to me by a dear friend in America, who has amazing gifts.

This person sat opposite saying absolutely nothing, not even the twitch of an eyebrow

. My friend had described–how precise is this for Heaven's sake! a stained glass window with a map of South America. At the end a languid admission to the accuracy of the session was made and a grudging mention of the window

I have actually suggested to people who do that that they leave since they don't obviously trust me. They get in a real state of anxiety in case I curtail the session.

When you are giving a massage, some drain you, others cooperate and the energy flows beautifully, both renewed.

I will not describe in any detail the politicians, who have been helped, or the police or the Forces but the gifts are to be used in all manner of circumstances, often to avert civil or military dangers.

Chapter 29

Recording

There are similarities between the medical profession and the world of the seer, the same ethics apply when someone close needs help. Many will not help their own families or friends fearing they may be emotionally influenced and it's a good safeguard.

However Love conquers everything and in my opinion when the need is overwhelming, help should always be given.

In my own experience a god child very dear to me asked about the chances of having healthy children, surviving pregnancy. Her child had not survived and a rare condition was found.

This was the hardest choice of my life to date. Would love cloud my judgment ? Which doctor would take such a chance? But there is no chance, only the fallibility of the seer if the emotions intrude.

So trusting the divine intelligences, she was told to proceed, all would be well.

As it turned out. Two beautiful children.

Tapes are very important in this work or cd's to record. There is healing in the session, so it can always be reactivated.. One guy told me he had listened to his for seven years which made me very happy. He needed a medical intuitive so I gave him the phone number of a very gifted person in the South West of England. He was so impressed he phoned me up to say.

'She told me to get a glass of water and put it by the phone. Then she told me I have lead poisoning, which is true!'

I was as excited as he was. Healers should always recommend clients to those they know who can give more specific help. No competition among healers.

In the States a loving mother was devastated by the behaviour of her son who was heavily into drugs. She couldn't eat, sleep, work; her life too was in ruins.

He was in prison and she was terrified he'd commit suicide.

Session

;This is where he had to be to learn. He has the path of a healer in a specific way.

Through the ingesting of drugs he has reached his lowest point. He will go into a programme which will cure him of his addiction and work with young people as a counsellor'.

She listened to the tape every day for a year she told me and it kept her sane and gave her hope and her son is helping others kick the same habit he had himself.

Chapter 30

Star People

There has been a recurring theme in the last seven years of my life. This will stretch the bounds of credulity but it is important that I write it. The point of these two books is to explain the life of a seer, that was the first and the second, the work of a seer. The application of the gifts in other words.

I have tried to give a wide cross section of the localities, the backgrounds of the querents, the gist of what each session gave.

Obviously if a session lasts around thirty to forty minutes there is a lot of information excluded for the sake of brevity here. And the energies affect people very much. Most will cry, even the Japanese men who do not like to show their feelings.

Seven years ago and the number seven has strong mystical and Biblical links seven days, seven rays, seventh child of a seventh child as my Irish grandmother was,.

I was in Axminster and a tall engaging American came to see me. From the beginning I knew she was like no one else, her energy was different, her vibration was different and the words came.

'You are from the stars'

She agreed and said no one else knew, but she did important work for the planet in helping avert natural disasters by working on grids.

Two days later I was in Southampton and there were a number of us in a large conference room of a hotel.

The door opened, a handsome tall man looked straight at me and headed directly over exactly as if we had an appointment.

He sat down looked at me and said,

'It's you I have to see.'

Straight away the words came.

'You are from the stars aren't you? 'Another star person.

He replied,

'I was told it was you I had to see.'

I scanned his health. He was living at too low an elevation, better for him to be on the top of a hill. He needed the colour green from minerals. I gave him my Moldavite.

I told him about the gyroscopic nature of the pulls around him and when I began to talk about the controller, he got agitated and said I was seeing too much so I stopped, out of respect.

I asked him if he knew any other star people in Britain and he said no but several in South Africa where he'd just left.

I phoned the American and asked if I could give her phone number to the South African so they could communicate. He was also here to help balance the gravitational pull, tornadoes and to curb the excessive weather imbalances. Quite simply, to help the planet.

I see them in a circle like the Save the Children logo hands clasped round the world.

From there to Australia, another woman, in a high government position in Canberra.

To the USA a native American Indian who also admitted to being one as the words came.

Back to Sydney a young man also from the stars, a brilliant healer.

On to Greece where a young Australian man admitted the same in a session that he was a star person and so was his partner. Both in high positions in the world of communication.

In Sedona, Arizona, another.

Most recently in New Jersey, a brilliant healer and teacher, female.

I have asked many other seers, practitioners.

'Have you met the Star people?' and the answer is always no.

And I have still no understanding of how the controller chose me.

And no understanding why I keep meeting them.

It will become apparent in time, I'm sure.

When I am ready to know.

Chapter 31

St Patrick's Night

From individual sessions, to group sessions and that is the way it seems to proceed. There seems to be a pyramid effect where healers start at the physical plane with aromatherapy, massage, manipulation of the body, touch, reflexology, Bowen technique and so on. Of course all the healing at that level effects the other planes too, just as the work on the subtle planes finds the area in the physical which needs healing.

From the physical plane usually the healer, seer moves on to vibrational healing or Reiki or sound healing which is a healing discipline which is really growing all over the world.

As the pyramid grows from working with dense physical to fine subtle energies in the aura, the same pyramid effect seems to occur in the working life of the seer, healer.

At the apex of the pyramid are those who have completed the seed planting in the lives of the people they've touched and have evolved into teachers, writers, healers of large masses, world influencing souls who recognize their higher mission.

Because this is a combined operation between the consenting seer, healer and the Higher forces operating for our highest good, the aura of the speaker touches the auras of those present, listening and it is of a very heightened vibration. Earlier I described the Russian woman who asked her question in Russian and I replied in English without knowing the question, and concluded that she might as well have been singing a nursery rhyme for if her intention was focused hat is all that's necessary.

In a sense, if we think of osmosis that is a fairly accurate description of what happens

Pop stars act magnetically on their fans who want to touch, be in physical proximity to their heroes. Then hysteria can set in.

When I was teaching in the east, I saw how this can spread like wildfire. If one female student fainted through stress, most of the others in close proximity did too.

Spiritually we are all one, no differentiation. The personalities like to pretend each is unique and in a sense that is true, it's a different combination of feelings, lived experiences and upbringing, but everything is one so what we do with our lives matters for the whole, as much as the individual!

It was in USA in Massachusetts that I was to give a demonstration of mediumship to an invited audience, who would dine as well as having me speak at intervals between courses!

I wore an emerald green silk chiffon blouse, to honour the Irish who would definitely be there, black trousers and red high heeled shoes to give me courage!

I was quite nervous not for the content of the evening, but because I had just flown in from the UK that day and was a bit dazed from the speediness of it all.

I was introduced and the buzz died down and the clatter of knives and forks stopped as everyone turned to look at me.

There are different ways of mediumship.I have watched painful displays where perhaps the audience was hostile, or the medium had a bad day, or the connection between the higher planes and our material world was not clear. And I have really suffered for the person who was floundering.

Also at healing weekends where large numbers are in close proximity, I have seen many examples of a message given out and perhaps six people in the audience have claimed it as appropriate for themselves. It seems to me that it's a bit like January sales, too many people wanting the same garment and a mad rush ensues.

Also in a heavily dominated Irish group, I think it was Saint Patrick's Day that I was the star turn, if a message from Mary came through, probably every hand would've shot up into the air!.

I decided to take the opposite route to opening the doors of the January sales and I'd use names instead and work upwards. That way there would be no mistakes, for in an individual session, there are no mistakes. If the person gives proof by some memory that only they and the person close to them know, there's no error.

As I looked at the diners they were curious, some friendly, some definitely hoping that

I'd fall on my face and a dead cert, they would take no prisoners. Mostly legal, medical and detectives from forensic.

It's funny what stays in your mind. I remember the cynical expression on the face of the barman who was polishing glasses with a cloth.

I took up my pen and a sheet of paper, did my preamble and the words came.

I moved, made eye contact, and engaged each part of the audience as I went from name to name. Fast, very fast. It was my intention to give something to every single person present. It's sad at the end of a demonstration that the guy next to us got something, but not us.

Session

'Your name, please, the lady in the pink cardigan? Marianne Branniigan?

At your shoulder there's a young man in military dress. You look at his photo very often.

The timing was wrong, only that.

...

The gentleman who has his back to the wall, trying to avoid my eyes. Your name?.Mark Adamson

You have an amazing opportunity just about to open for you. The person above you is taking a sideways move and this is your moment. Make a stand.

The blonde in the little black dress. Your name? Anne Flynne

There is an elderly person who took your mother's place. She loved looking after you and can't believe what you've attained Is so happy you gave your daughter her name.' (tears)

Fast, fast, fast!

There's total silence now. You could hear a pin drop. No skepticism now. The bartender is a frozen tableau, mouth open, white towel in hand. No circular polishing movement now!

'Remember, if I make any mistake you must speak up and tell everyone. I don't want you to rely on politeness. This is a demonstration about truth.

The girl in the violet dress. Your name?

'You have the same gifts as me. You are a very gifted healer. Believe in yourself'

Faster, faster, faster!

'Your name? Gentleman with the .beard. Keiran Hogan

You have a strong man right behind you. He looks like you. In your last very difficult situation, this man stood shoulder to shoulder with you. It wasn't your imagination, he was there.'(tears)

All round the room. No food served.

Everyone, and no one said that's not correct as I knew it would be. I have total faith in my helpers.

Last of all. The barman.

He jumped, for he didn't think he'd be included, not being a paid up guest! As if....

'You are a very intelligent man and your studies are waiting for you to pick up again You had no alternative to give up when you did, now's the time. Seize your opportunity.'

He nodded, dumbfounded.

Each was given what they needed to know. I didn't choose, select or eliminate.

Sometimes it was a past loved one. Sometimes a call to change their lives.

That was my baptism by fire, for there was no quarter given! They were very appreciative and bemused, really.

I couldn't eat. Too much adrenaline. Over a hundred guests.

I wonder why I knew there had to be no mistakes. It didn't come from pride. It came from the understanding that if it were impeccable, seeds would be planted in people's minds to investigate further

A very gifted medium I know with a great reputation in UK who teaches developing mediums told me of her experience in Spain.

I had described Saint Patrick's night to her.

She said about Spain,

'I've never felt anything like it before. There was alcohol and it felt as if I were trying to walk through mud. Out of ten attempts, I'd say I got three.'

This woman is tops in my opinion and it was valuable for me that she explained how even the best can be stymied by circumstances. It also showed her great honesty and humility.

There was a display at a healing centre and two mediums took the floor, one was to back up the other but actually the back up was stronger than the lead. The lead struggled, paced up and down, the back up was succinct and fast and accurate.

I went to a workshop on colour healing in London.

I was paired with a really sweet older lady who told me she was studying to be a medium and it had cost her hundreds of pounds in a college. I wanted to say,

'If it's not there why try and bring it forward when you have so many other gifts and talents?'

But I didn't, her choice

A healer, seer in the S.W..of England with a brilliant sense of humour told this great story in Wales at a healing workshop. We all had to say why we were there and I said,

'I want to be heal animals."

He told us that animals have no resistance to healing as people have for the cognitive aspect is missing. And that they give healing unconsciously, all the time.

Here was this great tale against himself, why he was so much loved, I guess.

He decided he'd write a book and that he'd become very wealthy indeed with this book.

He self published and mountains of books came to his tiny picturesque cottage.

He sold some, not as many as he'd thought and stored the rest in his loft.

The ceilings sagged and he had to get a joiner to come and lower the doorways for the doors could no longer open!

Moral of the tale, keep your expectations within bounds!

This seer was unable to shut down the process and so day and night without ceasing, he was in direct communion with higher forces. I've only met one other like that, a Cypriot man, an amazing soul who does great work as a healer, teacher and minister.

This instance I've given was the closest I've come to show biz. Had the opportunities, but I guess we're all pulled to what is right for us.

Quite soon after this experience in America I was taking part in a psychics' holiday and was asked to do a demonstration of mediumship.

The audience was made up of very old souls, those who had reincarnated many, many, times and had retained a lot of knowledge.

I knew this would be very challenging for they are so very talented themselves.

There were psychic surgeons, mediums, healers, clairvoyants, therapists, fifty in all.

As before in USA I felt strongly that each should be given something for themselves.

As before working from name up, everyone was included. One man, I know, did not want his to be imparted so I asked him quietly should I stop and he said yes.

This happened in New England some years ago.

I have a genuine wampum belt from an Indian tribe before Canada was Canada, given to a Scottish sculptor.

I took it to the States the first time I went there for it felt appropriate.

A TV crew came up and interviewed me about the provenance of the wampum belt and one said

'Show me what you do.'

So I asked his name and the words came.

I could not have said more than three sentences when I saw the look in his eyes and said,

'I think this is too private, don't you? 'A look of intense relief came over his face!

Chapter 32

Water

A seer relates closely to energies and the vibration of Nature and Nature spirits.

Sometimes it's the land itself which communicates. Mountains are sacred in many cultures, like Mount Fuji or Mount Kinabalu in Sarawak. In the same way that royal families carry the bonding of the land with the people who inhabit it, the lion in the jungle the king, the mountain 's energy stands tall in the kingdom of earth and minerals.

It is considered a desecration of the mountain to urinate there or spit. I always feel when in the mountains that I don't want to take a thing from them, even as far as taking a photo, I would first ask permission.

My father was way in advance of his time. A keen countryman, land surveyor his knowledge was formidable. Every tree, plant, grass he could name. He taught everyone in the family about the stars, the rivers, the mountains.. He was a walking encyclopedia about

Nature, history, ancient civilizations. From him and his father, the love of the environment grew.

As I traveled the world, it came to me that water being sacred and the planet's awareness of its growing importance increasing almost daily, that I should include this in my work.

So in every country I visited a sacred place. In Somerset went to Glastonbury to collect water, tinged red with the iron content of Chalice Well. Such a wonderful place to meditate in and see the majestic Tor towering above.

In Skyros, an island in the northern waters of Greece, on a walk, I found a natural spring where locals came with their empty plastic bottles.

In Australia water was collected from Perth, Sydney and Brisbane.

From USA, from Florida, collected from the Fountain of Youth where the early Spanish settlers met the very tall Indians and attributed their height to the water! This is in Saint Augustine.

From Lourdes some water. From Chimayo in New Mexico.

In Cyprus Cape Andreas from the sacred spring. From Saint Rafael's church in Cyprus, where miracles take place, some water.

This was then solarised in Cyprus, energized by me, crystals added and it is combined, bottled and labeled with flowers, for love, abundance and joy.

This desire to bring together the waters of the world, as we are one in spirit felt very important.

At this time there were influences around, where I'd gone to a lecture given by a Cypriot who had lived in the Rain Forest of South America for ten years. He was very shamanic in his approach and I found it fascinating. He showed slides of the spirits of the Rainforest which appeared when he turned his camera ninety degrees and the resulting pictures were truly amazing. Images of Hindu deities or Buddhist .bodisatvas were in the trees and mirrored in the water, Some seemed female, others animal like.

He didn't get a good reception.

Simultaneously I had discovered the work of Dr Masaru Emoto who wrote' The Hidden Messages in Water.'

This very important study shows that words and images have different effects on water which become visible in crystalline form when frozen. Love, beauty, kindness all form exquisite crystals, perfectly formed.

On the other hand, words like hate, violence and envy produced malformed crystals.

Since our body contains so much water the effect of cruel words and swearing affect us at a crystalline level, adversely.

I also believe although it hasn't been verified yet that the exposure to gratuitous violence and perversion in DVD's has a coarsening effect and lowers the vibrationary rate of whoever watches, whatever age.

And the fact that something crude and unnatural has entered the house via the media also remains in the vibration of the home.

There are certain authors who are extremely talented but whose work I won't read for I know it's coming from the dark side. Perhaps the authors themselves are unaware of this.

It leaves an almost tangible, dirty taste or smell, for evil smells, that's my physiological reaction anyway.

Recently two of us went to Salem. I took an aura soma essence with me, Archangel Michael.

I didn't go on any tours or visit any buildings, just sat and looked at the sea, its importance being established by the shipping connection.

Near the courthouse my throat began to feel very tight and constricted and a heaviness of spirit pervaded my senses. Those events of victimizing innocent women still cast a long shadow, from 1692 to 2009. But then, as said earlier, there is no linear time!

Watching the boats in the long harbour and thinking of the word Salem, derived from Shalom, peace, I sprinkled more of the Archangel Michael essence, discreetly as I had been doing since our arrival.

Water being a sacred element and in many world faiths used for purification purposes. it felt the right thing to do.

Mystic in Connecticut had wonderful energy. An artists' colony and sea port the sound of the deep hooter as the bridge swung open to allow boats to sail down the river will remain a vivid memory.

So places retain the stamp of what has gone before and sensitives and seers will pick up very easily the vibration of the place.

One of the schooners we sailed past in the harbour had the head of Joseph Conrad, who wrote' Heart of Darkness 'carved as its prow!

From collecting water, to using the voice as a healing tool, I recorded two CD's in the recording studio near by in Cyprus.

The musician, a very talented guy who is very aware himself, noticed that there was something different. He sensed that just before I spoke into the microphone, the instruments were picking up another frequency. I don't use a script, headings only and I'm in a heightened state while talking.

The first CD is called 'Healing through Visualisation' and it has been used fo r meditation by other healers and in group work and also people have told me they go to sleep while listening, that it alleviates loneliness and they use it to deepen their own spiritual journeying.

The second CD had to be about water, it was a natural sequel to the work of collecting water from distant places.

As the water's energy was part of my work as the seer, interested shamanically in the elements and earth's energies I made water and waterways the focus of this CD.

To honour the various continents and their own unique features, I chose a water which had truly inspired me.

The beauty of Australia and one of its many bridges is the subject of the front cover from a photo I took from East Balmain.I like the energy for whatever I make or see to be hands on, produced by me spontaneously. The cover of my book,' A Feather, Falling' was taken from a photograph of a feather from my Bruneian days, from the Great Argus Pheasant, the rarest bird in the world, which is only found deep within the jungles of Borneo and Malaysia.

The inside cover has a photograph of a beautiful horse and me in Cairo and the rose is the Damascus old rose which grows in the garden. Its perfume is overwhelming in the few short weeks that it blooms.

So the art work includes Cypriot energy, Egyptian energy, Australian energy and the CD the following.

Darling Harbour, Sydney. The energy here is busy, productive, beautiful and contains the heart energy of the city.

The lights in the evening shining on the water are a myriad of jewel bright colours.

The harbour, in contrast, of Hong Kong is mysterious and shifting because of the swirling mists that change the scene continuously. The nine dragons of Kowloon, the craggy mountains appear and disappear, hypnotically.

The waterway of a Scottish stream is icy cold, bracing, full of amethyst quartz and cold winds pull at you as you listen. This is to prepare you for the challenges of life.

Chesapeake Bay has the energy of the Native American Indians all around and the canoes of the young schoolchildren who learn water crafts there. There is a watching energy there and a combining of the past with the present in an indivisible, seamless way.

Aphrodite's bathing place evokes lambent greenish blue water of a secret grotto. Love is very evident here in this place and on this particular track.

Chalice Well, Somerset is all to do with healing and meditating under the Tor, the female and the masculine energies in close proximity.

Tintagel, Cornwall, is the final track and in this, we are in a boat which enters the crystal cave and with a guided meditation we receive a gift from the cave for our heart.

There are two stories connected with the making of this CD showing nothing is random in life!

The day before I was in Limassol, helping someone who was very bardic. Bardic is the adjective from bard, meaning a singer, poet, actor who is close to the Dionysian tradition of the sacred arts.

I saw a green dragon around this man and he was fascinated. When I am in the east, I often feel the presence of dragons, flying in around the aircraft before we land. Above the heads of gifted and ambitious people I see a red or gold dragon. Very occasionally above a woman's head and that is when she is an outstanding leader in her field or born in the Year of the Dragon.

On the day of the recording both the musician and I had a very tight schedule and the weather was wild. It thundered, sleet, lightning, high winds and torrential rain.

We spoke on the phone and decided we'd go ahead unless there was a power cut in which case the decision would be taken for us. This was a very unusual weather pattern for Cyprus at this time of year.

We began the session but just before the recording began, I said,

'I'm seeing green dragons here! I saw one yesterday, but they're all over.'

He smiled, saying,

'Come here,' and led me into the interior of his home, green dragons everywhere,

'I was born in the year of the dragon,' he said and it all made sense. The Dionysian energy of sacred art, dance and drama belonging to the green ray and the dragon energy.

We made the recording when the rain ceased and at the last, Tintagel track the storm increased. We kept on but it seemed to me that the elements themselves wanted to be on the recording! If you listen very carefully, for it's almost been edited out, but at my insistence you can hear the faint thrumming of the rain as you are in the boat, entering the crystal cave of the heart!

This experience reminded me of the similarities between things or synchronicities. The weather and the element water in a drought plagued island with empty reservoirs,

Cyprus.

The lecture of the divinities showing in photography of the Rain Forest and simultaneously seeing the crystalline images that form in water when a beautiful word or emotion is applied. In both, realities below outer manifestation.

Chapter 33

Geronimo!

The way that things open in the path of the mystic or seer is quite hard to describe

There's a knowing, in your bones if you like, that there's something you're required to do or study.

It seems to have a will of its own as you try to rationalise and say why this isn't a good idea, that the timing's wrong, there are so many bills to pay at this time and so on. But it doesn't go away.

If there was a great booming voice saying,

'This is what we want and the reason is...' there would be no test of faith.

And that is central to the whole process, faith, trusting that you are submitting to the divine plan.

For years I've seen it as being a soldier of light, Soldiers follow the path of duty. They put the good of the group before their own. They protect those weaker than themselves while teaching them to become stronger. They are brave in adversity. They use all of their skills and they keep their cool when the going gets tough. They are loyal and knowing fear, they still keep going.

In every seer's life that I know and they might call themselves mediums, clairvoyants, psychics, healers, whatever, those are the outstanding characteristics, they have faith and they have courage..

When they're asked to step out of the comfort zone of their safe, salaried profession, to give up the millionaire building business that they had, to live their lives simply, in unison, with that inner song which they follow all their lives, to be that mouthpiece or silver pipe of the kingdom of light, then that is their testimony, their gift of service to mankind. And it is inestimable.

In the poem by W.B.Yeats who brought out his spirituality through the beauty of verse,

Wandering Aengus searches all his life for the golden apples of the sun and the silver apples of the moon.

In allegory and metaphor we come closest to the truth. Interestingly I have been told that Greek is full of metaphor in comparison with English which lacks those poetic nuances.

I know that 'grandmother' in our ageist society is often used as an insult at football matches when the goalkeeper fails to keep the ball out of the net!

Here in Cyprus, Greek speaking,

'Grandmother….to have lived.'

Often the sacrifice that is inherent in following the path of the spirit has to do with giving up the material world. Obviously we must eat, pay bills but truly our needs are met by the Universe, our wants are not.

Sometimes it is giving up a sinecure to do something challenging. Leaving our home where we grew up for the impetus we need to bring out our gifts is not to be found there.

That is when we unconsciously challenge others in the group by our actions and they don't like it. We make them uneasy. Unwittingly we challenge their own choices.

In my own case, having been 'told 'that my mission was to leave Scotland and open doors for the family all over the world, it was the young, around twenty, and the elderly women in their eighties who were most encouraging. My own age group was shocked!

'Look what you are giving up!'

I had a promoted position in the academic world. We had a nine roomed Victorian villa. No one could understand that I was 'on orders.'

That was the time of giving up status and social position.

Afterwards giving up a privileged military teaching career with all benefits of NAAFI, free car allowance, free housing to retrain and go to Brunei to teach on the Water Village was another Geronimo moment.

In each case something had to be sacrificed in order for new growth to take place.

I believe I'm fortunate in that the material doesn't have any attraction any more, for the children are grown and their needs have been met.

Income comes and goes like the tide in all of our lives, sometimes high, sometimes low, the pattern will remain, but in relaxing into and honouring the Universe's infinite abundance, we enhance our lives, by not attaching to the end results.

There are some books and DVD's which have come out in recent years that are life changing and very important as beacons in our time.

'The Secret' has transformed people's thinking. I first saw it in USA in its original format when it first appeared. It blew me away and I bought five copies one for each of my children and myself.

The second,' Ask and it is Given 'by Esther and Jerry Hicks. That probably affected me even more than 'The Secret' I feel that it was given to mankind via these two gifted people who are at a very high spiritual level of development.

The third by Eckhardt Tolle,'The Power of the Now'

In exposure to all of these a change takes place through the experience. There is a quickening in the understanding of people and how they co create their own reality through the power of thought and intention. Visualisation is of course part of it, for the power of the imagination is boundless.

I've recommended these in every workshop, lecture and talk wherever my journeys have led me.

For this is a part of the weaving of the fife of the seer. As the paths criss cross through life in the journeys, all kinds of information and connections are made with the planet itself through walking the land, with the people we encounter and the animals.

In Verona park the meeting with a ground hog, an animal I've never seen before which would not leave me alone! I know its coming into my life is significant in what way I do not know. yet....the end of winter/ although he came to me in July! A change in some way in my life? It will become apparent.

I keep a diary. It's very brief. Often one word suffices. I'd recommend it to every one. If anything unusual happens, a dream, an unusual occurrence you can flip back. It's helped me on so many occasions to see a pattern that I wouldn't have noticed otherwise. I've done this all my life.

This is also helpful. When we have very busy lives and the day to day stops us doing what we want to do as spiritual beings in a material body, maybe daydream, a better word than meditation!

To go inwardly to honour our own individuality is hard to do in a family situation.

Someone always wants us. There are so many demands on our time. In our sleep our higher selves or guides, if that's an easier term, rather than helpers, or divine intelligences, or healers in the higher dimensions, work with us so that in our sleeping state we're growing spiritually.

One friend who has real gifts of the spirit has wonderful dreams of sea creatures, whales, dolphins as well as the saints to whom she has a special devotion. With three strong sons and husband and her own business that is how her spiritual life grows. By going on pilgrimages by sea to holy, healing islands in the Mediterranean she feels at one with her spiritual self.

So, last thing at night before going to sleep, ask your helpers to teach you what you need to know while asleep or if you need healing, ask for that. And remember to say thank you!

If we don't ask, we won't be given. Often healers are great at giving, not good at receiving. So we pray for those who are sick and forget to add ourselves into the equation. We deserve as much as we give to others, not more and not less.

The power of words is enormous. Never put out a negative comment or word. It's floating out there in your field and if you do it on a regular basis you bring your vibration down and quite probably your health.

These are 'forbidden 'words and phrases if you like!

'Things never work for me.' Pessimism

'I expect to fail my driving test.' You will...you've put it out there already!

'It's only me on the phone.' Low self esteem.

'Watch out...you'll fall. 'Your subconscious will hear fall and it will happen.

'I don't think my new boss likes me'. Another negative.

'Do I look horrible in this? 'Low self esteem and being in need of reassurance.

See yourself as beautiful, warts, bumps and all and radiate your self love.

Don't look for completion in another, find it within yourself.

Remembering the crystals from water, keep the thoughts strong so that no distortion takes place.

A scientist who is also a medical intuitive whom I met in England, told me that one of the personality traits she'd found in some cancer patients, is the inability to stand up for themselves.

I thought of those I knew who had succumbed to this disease and it was a fit.

So having boundaries in life is important for self esteem and also for good health.

It's impossible to deny the influence of the emotional plane on the physical structures.

That is one of the reasons that I was led to study flower essences and combine them with waters from all over the world.

Another of the pushes from behind!

I had already studied oils while studying Ayurveda while teachings in the east. I know they are fantastic agents of healing. and I use them daily.

The two I wouldn't be without are orange oil for optimism and lavender for calming and relaxing.

So the seer who is also the healer (and the reverse is true,) uses energy and vibration to effect change in the planes, If one is doing a session and scans, using the crystalline lens in a specific way towards health, a pattern may appear which is jumbled. For example, say, a finger caught in the door will have all the molecules rushing around in all directions.

I have seen the power of sound heal in this case while a group of people sang a sustained vowel, directing it to the finger. With higher sight, all the molecules looked like they were being combed back into order! It was fascinating.

Session

Scanning the body from the top of the head downwards.

Tightness across the chest and blockage at the throat centre.

Sleeplessness and pain in the head, Loss of libido.

Ways of helping would be to use rose oil in the bath, a few drops only. This would help heal the emotional heart.

Immediate feelings of the containment of grief at recent loss.

Writing for very private people a letter for themselves only to read would release suffering and the letter subsequently to be destroyed.

A lessening of constriction at the throat would follow.

To counteract sleeplessness, there are two methods.

One is to exercise vigorously an hour before going to bed, dance, jogging, yoga.

Run a bath and put lavender drops in.

Boil four lettuce leaves, any kind, in a small pot covered with an inch or so of water,

Bring to the boil and simmer for ten minutes and drink the water with or without honey.

Second is to hold a mineral sphere in your hands till it gets warm. This can be rose quartz or any quartz and hold it till it becomes warm. As you feel the warmth your body becomes sleepy. And put it under your pillow it will carry on working as you sleep.

When general health picks up libido naturally returns.

The vibration of water is high, oil is denser, a lower note.

Because of my work with water worldwide and using it as the focus of my CD's it seemed appropriate to add flower essence healing to the mix. for the energy of flowers is very high.

We all love going into a garden centre and feel healed just by walking through the paths and seeing the colours, inhaling the scents, and brushing against the various herbs and leaves.

Since this is high potency and frequency healing at the emotional level, it can cause a reaction as the release takes place. People might feel tearful Since we resonate most strongly with the plants in the area in which we were born, temperate zone felt right for me. As I travel I see wonderful bush remedies in Australia. In China, ancient Chinese flower remedies, for example chrysanthemum petals for coughs and colds and chest problems. In S.E. Asia rajah bunga flower for chest problems also in Japan. In Sedona desert remedies so choosing was difficult.

The course I studied comprises four types, Bach, North American, Alaskan and Master flower remedies.

From my travels in India I know the purest flowers are to be found in Kashmir where they had herbalist training centres centuries ago. Pansies, roses, lavender, lilies, cornflowers all grow there in profusion, scenting the air.

So certain emotional conditions are helped by flowers as Dr Bach discovered in his important work in the nineteen thirties. For example holly as an antidote to jealousy.

Honeysuckle for homesickness. Fear there are many types of fear, phobias, f ear of losing the beloved, each has its own flower remedy to be taken by dropper as often as required.

It feels that the planet needs to raise to a higher frequency now. If we are continuously evolving, our bodies and subtle bodies will evolve too, seeing food absorption altering as we become a finer species.

Germany has a n excellent health programmer where people, who are run down are sent to areas to recuperate which suit their condition.It might be they are sent to a lake with trees around. Someone else might be sent to the mountains for the scent and healing of pines.

Others to a hot water spa. others to the sea. Altitude and humidity factors are taken into account

This seems so very wise. People and the environment working in harmony, instead of imposing our pattern on things.

I often imagine the mother, the earth, our first mother, since from her all creatures came, as the fields of corn her billowing hair, the streams and rivers her arteries and the mountains her bones.

Chapter 34

Psychic Surgery

In the categories of workshops that I undertake in different cultures I try to make them as interactive as possible. The result hopefully at the end of the session will be that everyone's gifts are seen, recognized and developed in some way.

I am often asked to do workshops to develop intuition and this is very enjoyable. Lots of us think we can't do things when we can.

One psychic surgeon told me over lunch one day that he has no other faculties, heard nothing, saw nothing just got taken over by a Scottish surgeon and remembered nothing

We watched him work on someone with a bad shoulder. Five of us compared notes afterwards..B saw in colour. Ksaw the implements. C saw in black and white like me and M saw in colour also.

The shoulder went faster and faster then detached like a doll whose arm can come out of the socket and be replaced. The patient got up, in tears as he realized there was no more pain.

There was no question of chicanery. He is absolutely genuine as were all the people present there.

At an evening gathering, we all had to do something that we didn't usually do. Mine was psychometry which is something I do occasionally but not a lot. The surgeon had to describe my mother from her name and he was completely correct and was elated!

In Hong Kong the groups spoke good English and were all fairly sensitive but didn't believe in their own gifts.

Session

Greeting

General introduction

When we use our intuition…choosing foods our bodies need in the supermarket.

Exercise. Draw on the given sheet of paper in your mind only, concentrate. Hold the image. Fold it up and put your initials on it. Put it into a box with the others.

Randomly they choose one by one and open the sheet they've chosen.

Sometimes closing their eyes, sometimes not, they sense the picture and describe what they see.

In almost every case they got it right. Now some of that may be the heightened energy because of the group situation or it may not. One person didn't see but felt the emotion of the one who drew, which was also impressive. She saw an aircraft and the person had just flown in the previous night so that energy was strongly around her.

The important aspect of these workshops is that those who attend see their own potential; it's not about me but them.

I did an experiment and told them it was the first time I'd ever tried this and did they wish to cooperate.

When I was in Wales at the healing course the person leading it found an old black Victorian three sided box, upstanding. A person would sit inside on a chair and with the power built up from the audience, transfiguration would take place. Transfiguration is blending of spiritual essence with the person who is the medium. The face changes. A woman's face might resemble a burly bearded man's. A man might change into a pretty girl. It's very interesting to watch.The person in the chair has his eyes shut, but as you watch in the darkened room, eyes suddenly open as the spirit settles into that space.

Everyone saw the manifestation. Each person had a turn in the chair and I could speak at the same time as the transfiguration took place. when it was my turn. Usually you can do one. I know a very gifted healer who does both. They told me I became a wise oriental gentleman in a silk robe with long nails and spoke in a very scholarly way.

My plan was to see if we could dispense with the black three sided box and simply use a chair in a slightly darkened room. with total novices.

First blessed the room, burned sage to clear, said the words

'I work in light

I work in love

I work in truth.

Please protect us.'

And with a semi circle of chairs and a volunteer in the middle, the session began.

The woman who volunteered was definitely a sensitive.

Someone said,

'I can see eyes flickering!

Another said,' I can't' then,' Oh yes I can !'

Everyone could do the transfiguration and everyone could see, some faster than the others.

It was an amazing experience and they were thrilled with their success.

I closed the circle with thanks and again cleared the room and with a question and answer session to ground them, that is very important, we all felt we had learned a lot!

It might be asked, what the point of a demonstration of that kind is.

It takes away the mystique of the person who is leading the workshop and that is good. It is not a demonstration of their gifts but the students 'gifts and giving them a tangible reality. They could manifest and see others manifest, therefore it is not a gift that few have, but everyone has. Seeing is believing!

I was quite apprehensive in case nothing happened but how totally wrong I was!

In Florida I was addressing a large group of people, teaching skills and techniques for leading a more satisfying life, for I have been told, and believe it to be true that a large part of my spiritual path is to help women fulfill their potential and be stronger.

I think that is why I taught in an Islamic state and am now living on an Island where men dominate. However I am no feminist and help many men equally.

This group was intelligent also and had very good careers. Although it was to be more of a debate, my seeing kicked in and one by one I went round the group giving help and what they required.

One young woman was given her spiritual mission which was so powerful, involving local then national politics; she really is a woman of Destiny. She burst into tears and said,

'I so needed to hear that. I've always felt it even as a child.'

On that day her life changed.

Seers all say this. There are moments when you know that Destiny has stepped in at that moment and we are the instruments. All sessions are important but some are life changing.

At this time and place there was a very brave mother whose son had just died. She was truly remarkable and her son who came back to speak to her with his untidy beach shoes gave very good testimony. His friends were devastated but with this group, I really saw how important it is, that proof of life after death is so essential for those who grieve. This beautiful young man, so goodhearted and generous to everyone, had touched so many lives and was plucked away so quickly. The pain was very raw.

Chapter 35

Agros

Today I decided to take a break from writing and replenish by being close to Nature.

My friend had just experienced in the previous month a shocking bush fire which almost consumed them, their dogs and the house. And all ten acres of land were devastated.

I set off at seven am. with the cooler bag to buy ice en route for the temperatures are so very high, but ran back to get my car insurance details which I never do.

The tank was almost empty and being Sunday no service. My twenty euro note got swallowed, I must have pressed the buttons in the wrong sequence. The next two notes worked.

Having left a note with registration number saying 'I'll come in tomorrow for the twenty euros' I bought the ice and drove along the beautiful coast road past Aphrodite's birthplace, a place loved by people the world over.

Cyprus is a healing island and in ancient times, ships came from all over the known world to worship at her shrine in Geroskipou, which means garden of apples. The apple tree was sacred to the Celts and the Druids for the energy is so young and joyful.

As I drove, I spoke in my mind to the goddess, patron of Cyprus, goddess of love. This island is Taurean and Aphrodite or Venus in the Roman Pantheon, rules this island.

Further along the coast at Episcopi there is quite different energy. It is male and very powerful This temple is sacred to the god Apollo Hylatis, god of the woodland, herbs and healing in this instance. He is also the god who drives the chariot of the sun, the god of beauty and music. When you walk in the grounds of the temple, a vast complex near Curium, you brush against rosemary, basil and lavender and thyme, all the sacred healing herbs which grow wild there.

But today I joined the motorway, thinking of the worship of the old ones.

I stopped to buy a Sunday paper and had a coffee skerto without sugar and a tall glass of water, sitting under the vines sacred to Dionysios., god of wine and drama..

It felt great to be there under a green canopy, cool from the glare of the brazen sky, knowing I had loads of time to get to Agros in the Troodos mountains which was our destination. Village of roses. In May, the Damask roses come out at the same time as the wonderful cherry harvest of Pedoulas.The scent of this rose overwhelms the senses. I t blooms for a short time only, is like a bigger version of our wild rose and is deep lilac pink. It grows in my garden and its photo is on my website and CD cover. I love its fragility, its impermanence, the very Zen nature of this flower which lives fully in the moment!

Resuming the journey, the road to Agros climbed and climbed, twisting around what were obviously old goat tracks made into minor roads. Charming villages with vines and elderly people sitting in their doorways, so typical a scene.

The hotel where we were to meet I found easily enough, a little way out of Agros to avoid all the cars and locals getting the last enjoyment out of their long summer holiday.

I took a picture of the church outlined against the blue, blue, sky and bought a local delicacy, home made ice cream and sat under a fig tree, looking at the pomegranate orchard close by.

That triggered thoughts of Persephone, kidnapped by Pluto, ruler of the Underworld,

Hades and how Demeter her mother wept for her lost daughter and the earth suffered.

She ate only six seeds of a pomegranate while in Hades, hence six cold months of the year for she had to stay one month for each seed.

Pomegranates are seen here as symbols of fertility and given at Christenings and weddings as suitable gifts.

The reason for the trip to Agros, as well as social, was to buy fruit that you can't get in Cyprus. A very enterprising Cypriot couple, restaurateurs went to Poland and bought canes of raspberries, blackberries and blueberries which are now thriving n their small plot of land near Agros and they sleep under the stars with their fruit, twice a week, when they harvest it.

A labour of love.

We were given our kilo each of beautiful blackberries and raspberries which we put into the cool bags and drove to the rose factory which I've wanted to do for years.

The scent of rose products filled the air. Rose water and rose creams for the skin. Rose candles in the shape of roses and butterflies. Rose liqueurs and wines. Rose tea and potpourri, rose jam and pictures of the lovely damask rose.

With our purchases we made our way to the little shop nearby which sold walnuts in syrup, little pots of cherry, strawberry and quince jam.The quince is thought to be the golden apples of the Hesperides in classical literature. Homer spoke about the ancient culture of Cyprus which predates ancient Greece. I bought some of everything for the little pots make nice gifts and not many people like to drive in the hottest month of the year, very sensibly!

We found a little taverna which had local food and he reeled off the menu, nothing printed.

The story of the fire was recounted and the heroism of the firefighters. The local man who rang the church bell to waken the other villagers to go and help...this was at midnight. The men who fought the fire till dawn and went straight to work with no sleep or time to change.

The heavy feeling of presentiment which made her feel unwell and go to bed very early with a torch.

Her husband's excellent hearing when the bell tolled. and the voices shouting for them to leave.

From the coolness and beauty of the rose factory to the terror of that night. My friend who has worked so hard for animal welfare is sure she was looked after on that occasion.

.Quite definitely.

And so the long drive home with all the gifts of abundance from a fertile land which paradoxically suffers continuously from drought. The tap roots. must be very deep.

Deeply content, I arrived back in Paphos to hear a giant bang and the car wobbled, A blow out, a tyre gone and a great thankfulness that in the wild mountains it hadn't happened, for who would have known where to find me. Thanking whatever kindly guide for telling me to take my paperwork, it was a quick matter for the guys to change the wheel. It took their combined strength to unlock the screw threads.

So a Zen day, of many fragments, emotions, memories, classical studies and fruit to share in the village.

Brain refreshed to pick up the narrative!

Chapter 36

The Coming

The way that we perceive in the east and west is different. Western thought is more direct and rational. Eastern thought is more lateral and subtle. We are concerned with doing, the east with being.

One of the differences that I noticed in the media in the east, in the film industry, when they are portraying supernatural beings, they make them glide and they seem to be cut off at the knees! One Chinese friend said she really preferred western ghosts for they were so much more credible. Another feature that differs in the east is that they see guides or spirits who protect families as huge.

One of my friends told me how her grandmother saw portents before my friend was born.

Standing at the end of the longhouse where they lived in the Rainforest was a tall man, higher than the roof of the longhouse with a staff in his hand and he told her grandmother that this was a chief coming into the family and to prepare suitable foodstuffs to celebrate.

Dutifully she baked the cakes with the correct colours in preparation for the birth.

When the child was born, a female it made no difference, this was the chief as foretold.

Later when she was about sixteen and seriously ill, her door opened and in came the Herculean figure, the old lady dressed in olden days dress with a belt of silver coins and they sat on her bed, healing her.

She is important in putting forward the needs of the Ibans, especially women, in her writing, radio broadcasts and lectures so she is fulfilling her Destiny for herself and her people. as her grandmother had seen.

Later as I have described before at the blessing of her studies at an Australian university, these figures were standing behind her in the light, seen by me, a western seer, and Lunut an eastern seer.

There is also a fairly major difference in thinking about ill fortune that enters everyone's life at some point. The loss of a partner, or demotion, of being made redundant —all of these are challenges to be overcome.

In other societies there is a strongly held belief in the power of ill will directed towards one.

This is seen as the evil eye in Greece. In Malaysia it is seen as a spell put on one and it has to be removed. In Japan malevolent forces are seen as very real.

Oils are used in the creating of an attack on someone and in the removal.

I have never studied any of this, nor wish to, so I will simply say it exists and it's the power of the mind of the person who believes he/she is a target that gives it potency.

But here are some ways of protecting yourself from any adverse situation.

The first was taught me at an expo where I was surrounded by jealousy. A healer came up to me and said she could feel it so strongly, so we went to the ladies' room where no one would see us and this was what she showed me. It works, a hundred per cent.

Standing straight (with the left hand throughout) hand to left hip. Hand straight above the midpoint of the head, down to right hip. Up to left shoulder, touch then to right shoulder, touch and back to touch left hip.

You have inscribed a star of light on your auric field and with these words, nothing can penetrate that would harm you.

The words are to be said aloud.

'Elohim of the violet flame, take away anything negative.

Archangel Michael, protect me.'

Even as I typed these words onto the computer, I felt the energy lift.

Do this daily, as a routine, like brushing your teeth or taking your shower.

This works in boardmeetings, when there is jealousy around or you feel uncomfortable but don't know why. We are all vulnerable beings.

The second is using visualization to put oneself in a protective enclosed space. It might be inside a crystal but the feet must be within the crystal and the top of the head also.

The next is to buy a shield which has crystals inside the outer metal case. They are biomagnetic and stop the field of your mobile, your computer, or aircraft engine disturbing your own electro magnetic field. They need to be solarised every few days by being put out into the sun and never worn during the night.

People have of course the belief that a crucifix is powerfully protective and many miraculous stories are found in many cultures.

In the Islamic tradition, a verse from the Koran is rolled up into a tiny scroll and worn.

Each faith has its own beliefs which are to be respected.

In Cyprus grandmothers burn olive leaves to cleanse the house if, for example, a daughter in law with daughters has visited at the same time as a daughter with sons.

There would be no reason not to add the first star protection even if another symbol were worn.

Last thing at night, it is good to ask the guides, angels to heal and teach during the sleeping hours.

In my autobiography I described an occasion when a Chinese lawyer and his wife were pursued by a being attached to the roof of the car and the fact that the gates to their home had been blessed was enough to keep this entity at bay.

Intention is everything. An item which has been blessed regardless of the faith should be treated with respect, never thrown out with rubbish. Burned preferably.

Ritual is the same. Any waters that have been used or oil should be disposed of thoughtfully and with respect.

I keep returning to intention.

We see people who have received terrible injuries and they return to almost normal lives with the power of the will and the power of intention.

They can visualize it so strongly that the body obeys.

The reverse is also true. When the mind chooses for the body not to be well, that's the conclusion.

While studying Ayurveda in Brunei I learned a great deal and always had my file on hand to make notes.

In the healing place, where this amazing Brahmin Indian gave healing, freely, for many years while teaching, simultaneously. there were many instances of that.

When the will to be well was a strong feature, healing followed. And when there was weariness, lassitude in the eyes the healing passed by.

One lady who had been in a wheelchair for many years with joints badly affected by rheumatism in her early forties, followed the regimen given with baths and diet and massage all contributing to her healing. In a wonderful example of easrtern and western medicine in combination, for she had surgery to remove spurs of bone which impaired her walking she became fully mobile again after seven years in a wheel chair. What a success story!

When I was asked to study I was told to forget my higher gifts and start from the level of mixing oils, learning massage, clearing up and so on. I was glad to, for it was a once in a life time opportunity to study with this man. Hands on was exactly right!

Of course this was service again, the constant of the number seven ray.

Over the years I learned down to earth remedies from the kitchen cupboard, costing nothing and have been happy to share these wherever I go.

Here with you, also.

For arthritis, both types, massage the affected part with a light oil to get the circulation going.

In a small pot put two inches of peeled, chopped root ginger into water so the level is about an inch above the ginger. Boil and then simmer for ten minutes.

Wringing out a facecloth in the now yellow colored ginger water, as hot as you can bear, apply the cloth over the affected limb and cover with a towel which you wrap around to keep the heat in. Leave it for ten minutes.

Do this every second or third day.

Simultaneously drink ginger tea on a daily basis. Peel and chop two inches of root ginger and put into a teapot. Pour in boiling water and leave for five minutes then drink with or without honey to taste.

To bring down blood pressure and cholesterol peel a clove of garlic, bite it in two, swallow down without chewing to avoid breath odors with two tablespoonfuls of apple cider vinegar mixed with hot water and honey. Do it daily.

One guy in Connecticut made me cry. He told me a doctor in the hospital he attends had phoned him to find out why his count had gone right down! When he told him, the doctor said,

'I'll pass that right on to others with the same problem.'

Sometimes you wonder if anyone is really paying attention or not!

For headaches or migraines, cut a lemon in half and massage the temples in a circular movement to bring relief.

For sleeplessness as I wrote earlier in this book, five lettuce leaves boiled in a small amount of water and the water drunk before going to bed. Lettuce is a natural narcotic. Interestingly, a gypsy cure for sleeplessness too.

For PMT or PMS cinnamon bark tea, breaking four inches of cinnamon bark into a teapot, pouring in boiling water, leaving it to sit for five minutes and drinking with or without honey.

For acne or teenage spots acidophilus yogurt applied directly to the skin and washed off in the morning, nightly, till the condition has disappeared.

For flatulence a pinch of asafetida, heng in Middle Eastern terms, in cooking, tasteless with a nasty smell alleviates the condition.

For kidney stones, drinking star fruit juice daily helps dissolve them.

For stomach ulcers drinking cabbage water is very helpful.

Taking responsibility for our own health as far as possible is, I think, the best way to be, with of course medical help when needed.

These years of studying, learning, doing massage on a daily basis of perhaps six people with different problems was life changing.

In seeing others cope with pain, anxieties, it got one's own problems into perspective.

One night late in the evening, a Chinese lady came for healing. I was asked if I'd stay behind to help the healer and said I would. Coincidentally it was the occasion of the Sultan's birthday party and I had planned rushing home to shower and get ready in a relaxed way.

That plan was ditched. This lady was possessed and you could see the malignity come into her eyes. I was asked did I know what was wrong and answered yes.

Two is better than one in these cases. So we worked together till the eyes returned to normal. Over time she regained her health, physical and spiritual.

And I made it to the large party, for over four thousand people, slightly out of breath but not noticeably! Choices, always choices….

Chapter 37

Psychism v. Spiritualism

People think that being psychic is the same as being spiritual. It is not.

Being spiritual has everything to do with your ethics, the desire to help people, to realize there are worlds beyond our own and that hopefully we are progressing in refining ourselves so that our vibration is higher as we leave life than the level we were at when we entered. That our lives have been lived in thinking of others and being unselfish.

Being psychic may be that we are born with certain abilities that may or may not be part of our spiritual life.

Often they can be a bit like marsh gas that used to lead travelers from the correct path, the safe one into the marshes and quagmire.

They really are not that important. Party tricks.

In England recently I met an outstanding woman. I knew immediately that she was extraordinarily advanced spiritually and simultaneously with a brilliant mind.

I knew she had to be working in a very specific way and she gave very guarded responses. I think we shocked each other in a way. She hadn't expected me to see so far.

I hadn't expected to find someone at such a high level of spiritual development.

Her role in British Intelligence must be of enormous importance to the country. It made me happy to think that such a soul had incarnated to protect us.

To return to psychism, imagine you had a very good skill and people were amazed. You could utilize that and give up your hard working job to say, just wander around India, able to tell people's names just from looking at their faces. That is a fact by the way.

But what is the point? How have you helped people attain a higher level? Wouldn't it be better to farm the land, produce food to feed people?

So the attaining of psychic gifts is a waste of time unless they spring into life unbidden a s a result of following the spiritual path.

This is a true story. Many people struggle to learn how to astral travel. They fast. They meditate. It becomes an obsession.

Every night we all go astral traveling so wouldn't it be good to just leave it there when we do it naturally? All that energy!

One of my cousins with the same inherited gifts from the maternal grandmother told me this story which still makes me smile.

He went to a yoga class to learn to relax for he had a high powered position which caused stress.

At the end of the session, lying in the corpse pose as the whole class was doing, he left his body, stood at the side and saw himself lying there.

Somehow he got back.

At he end of the class he went to the teacher and said, in shaking tones,

'I came out of my body and saw myself lying on the mat!'

She looked at him with total amazement and said,

'People spend their whole lives trying to attain that, and you do it at your first yoga session!'

He replied,

'And I'm never coming back!'

And he didn't, but spends a lot of his time doing good works. And golf!

The magician in the tarot pack wears bright colours. The hermit a cloak of brown.

I was invited as a guest by a friend to the beautiful home of Uri Geller. She had bought a bent spoon for charity and was invited to an afternoon event with up to four friends. I was one of the four.

It was a very happy occasion and we saw the exquisite works of art and giant crystal geodes, which were my favorite, in the hall.

Someone of course pulled out a spoon and it was stroked and bent into a weird shape.

Someone else pulled out a spoon and this time it bent but not so much. The third hardly at all. It was a good example of power surges and then it diminishing.

I actually had never realized that people producing spoons could be part of a person's life in inappropriate ways!

He was very kind, for hearing that my son was to be married the next day in Scotland which was just a passing remark, he asked one of his helpers for a felt pen and autographed my suitcase with a message of good will, actually asking for their names and date of the marriage. That really impressed me, his spontaneity and generosity of spirit.

Thinking of the man who can tell anyone's name reminded me of a recent email. The organizer of the Australian expos has a feed back sheet, an excellent idea for it keep s standards high. In his email he said,

'Ignore the first comment…she expected you not to have to ask her name! 'I laughed. so had he!'

Maybe we should do a feed back on our clients!

I always tape sessions as I've said before. I t is so important for so much information is given. It's impossible to take everything in. Even years later people will find a nuance they missed.

One of the down sides of taping is that we use a very high frequency in our work. As the power builds electrical power surges happen. Light bulbs explode. Videos suddenly begin with no one pressing the automatic control. Clocks stop or mysteriously fast forward or go backwards.

And the taping process is not exempt from phenomena.

Naturally people suspect we didn't switch on properly. That the tape was incorrectly put into the machine. That it was a faulty tape. That we did something wrong! But truly these recorders are like a top cricketer's bat, we take care of our tools.lovingly

We should do a disclaimer saying

'To the best of our knowledge the tape will come out correctly but there are times they won't.' The importance of the session is the information you are given…. the tape is an optional extra.

Here are some true examples.

Three women came to see me in Cyprus. British.

Three tapes were made and I tested them all at the beginning of the session, counting one, two, three, and playing back the recording.

At the end the first came to me with a grin. We heard the numbers and dead silence. The other two were perfect. She said,

'I actually didn't want mine taped.'

Her intention of not taping, I believe, affected the recording.

On another occasion, a sensitive part dealing with emotions, faded away to become inaudible and when that part of the session finished back came the full clarity and volume.

On other occasions a third voice is heard. Usually when it's mediumship. In the States one woman brought the tape back for me to listen. Two of us in the room, her voice and mine and a man's saying,' No' this was in reply to a rhetorical question during the mediumship session with her father. Clearly as ours.

I was sending a tape to UK the only one on the coffee table. I listened to both sides, sent it and it was blank.

Very often when there are two healers or seers in a room it acts like two north polarities in a school science experiment with magnetism. They can reject the particles.

This is so well known a phenomenon that healers and seers together don't even talk about it. We know it is a fact of our lives. We are not in charge of the recordings, our guides are, and they select what is appropriate or should be eliminated.

I am always amused by the suspicious nature of journalists who do not want tapes, thank you, and gather up the tiny bits of papers with their names as if they are gold dust
. Sometimes I challenge and say,

'If there is a lack of trust I'd rather you leave."

An embarrassed denial always follows. If we are not scrupulous in our intention to help with our gifts, they would be taken from us, quite simply.

Many think we are in a very advantaged position and can use our gifts to help us solve the problems we encounter.

That is an impossibility. We are not allowed to use our gifts for ourselves. We cannot, for our wants and desires would cloud the lens.

If we get the information we need in our sleep state that is genuine usually, if it comes in a meaningful dream, or vision, bypassing the conscious mind, But not in an ordinary dream for often they give the opposite,. the old saying,' Dreams go by opposites is true.

We can't be detached about our own problems.

Our emotions colour everything. If we don't show them enough, we're thought to be cold.

If we show them too much we are seen to be weak. Often the advice given to women in court cases is not to be emotional, to have words ready that impress with their objectivity and detachment.

You will always win in a situation where you have the advantage of the unexpected.

Sadly a stereotypical attitude towards women is that they resort to tears. Then the mental plane person has the winning hand for he feels nothing.

That is equally true when it is the man who is emotional and the woman coldly appraising.

If it seems to be too difficult, imagine you are acting a part of someone who has iron self control and detachment. It works.

Someone in a very difficult situation, intelligent beyond his years, explained how he hated to be patronized in company.

Some phrases were given.

To remove a hand on a shoulder ...'Watch the threads! 'With a smile, reinforcing street cred..Always with a smile.

I think this is inappropriate, don't you?

I have been personally in situations where cruelty, when one was a victim of circumstances was not infrequent.

I always used laughter and the person would be perplexed.

'Why doesn't she react to the barb? 'So as not to give satisfaction, obviously!

I was giving a demonstration once to a large group. Half way through I halted to think how to put, in a good way, what the next person needed. I knew that this particular medium would heckle me. The gap was maybe five seconds.

Sure enough, up she piped,

'Dried up, have you? '

I was prepared.

'Just testing and you were as predictable as usual'

.The company laughed with me and I carried on, seamlessly.

We may be spiritual but we also have to honour ourselves and have our boundaries of what's acceptable.

I was taking part in a yoga class in my twenties in Scotland. One of our friends, a doctor's wife, was being looked at in a very hostile way by one of the older doctors' wives. I could feel it so badly and something hurtful was said.

I felt the energy ball up to get my friend, intercepted it and threw it back where it came from. All the lights went out.

I would not do that now for I understand that even though it wasn't coming for me and I was protecting someone else, it should have been intercepted and put into the ground, deeply, to render it harmless and seal it over. That is what I would do now. Neutralise what is negative, not feed it with one's own indignation.

All of this took place at the invisible level but it was tangible though invisible.

Another example of invisible energy having a tangible effect. I was studying art and there was a student who felt deeply for the teacher. I t was not reciprocated.

The tension grew higher. Easels broke, not longitudinally along the grain, but straight across. Many.

A wise man in London deduced immediately why the energy bottled up was acting in this bizarre way.

. It stopped as quickly as it began.

The power of our thoughts, which are things, is immense.

It is so easy when things disappoint us to mull over and over. It's like a stone which is worn away by water.

We long for the beloved, maybe a soldier far away and we can't eat or sleep. Friends tell us to buck up, keep busy and the mind remains fixated on what it cannot have through circumstances beyond our control. Doesn't stop us though. We play the same scene over and over.

We've all been there.

I often think if the power of all the yearning in the world were put together we would have no more use for fossil fuels! We could drive all the machinery in the world with it.

And what good does it do?

What use does all the worry in the world have? What can we change with it? The bills that are impossible to pay, say, three coming together cannot be paid with the energy created by the worry. If we stop worrying, replace it with action which is fire, face the bills and say

'I can pay so much this month and the rest next."

then there is a resolution to the problem. When we feel our hands are tied and we can't act, then the negative cycle truly takes over, for we have handed over our power to those who have sent out the bills.

Worrying creates health issues one of which is gastric problems in the stomach and irritable bowel syndrome.

So a strategy which works with repetition. is this.

See your situation as a game of chess.

If it is an emotional issue then you know the water element is imbalanced. So you use fire to balance.

Fire at the mental plane is thought, at the physical is action.

When the mind is drawn towards sadness or grief, see the chess piece that you need and either exercise vigorously by going to the gym, playing tennis, doing aerobics or studying something that interests you.

To take the image of snooker, play the shot against the table so it ricochets and reaches its goal. The dynamic of the energy changes the reaction.

The fear of failure can act as a spur to heights undreamed of. Everything can be used as a dynamic of change.

The misery of a bad job can spur us on to restudy, emigrate. or become self employed.

The misery of an affair ruining a young family can cause the mother to become more powerful as she realizes she is capable of keeping her family in safety by her work and her strength.

Chapter 38

Karmic Love and Survival

Some of the biggest challenges in life are caused by the love aspect of our lives. No one is going to pretend it's easy. We can be torn apart by the force of our emotions
. Intelligence flies out the window. Rational thinking, a thing of the past.

I am going to spend a considerable amount of time in this book on the love aspect for in the work of a seer, all human conditions are met. This does not mean I have the answers.

I am as vulnerable as the next person, but the vast body of experiences encountered may be of help.

If we belong to the mental plane and are analytical, finding the cognitive part of the brain easy and the affective, or emotional and creative part difficult, we can be very controlling if we are in a relationship with an emotional person. It doesn't matter which way round it is, male mental, female emotional or female mental and male emotional. the problems are the same.

The mental plane partner can always push the buttons of the emotional partner.

The analogy is often given in this way.

Imagine that the mental plane partner has the capacity to feel (water) to fill a tumbler to the brim.

Imagine the emotional plane partner has the capacity to feel (water)to fill a gallon container.

When the mental pours all the content of the water in the tumbler into the gallon container it will probably reach four centimetres up the sides of the gallon container.

When the emotional person fills the tumbler from the gallon container overflows fifty times There is a basic disparity here

As said earlier, an elephant can not comprehend the way of the lynx.

There is nothing wrong with either.

In an ideal world the mental plane people would meet and fall in love and the emotional or water plane people would meet and fall in love. Both would understand the other for they would be in balance.

If we could fully grasp that concept a lot of the feelings of hurt and pain would disappear.

Women are very supportive of each other usually when it's about feelings.

Men always seem to be slightly bemused and want to be lighthearted and jokey whether mental plane or emotional plane. for it's an image issue.

Recently a good friend told me of something that had hurt her. Her partner had not responded to a situation in the way she thought he should..

I, the outsider, could see both points of view. but it was a friction point which went deep.

One is more sensitive than the other in some ways though the other is too but not on that evening. It was actually socially adept to handle it the way he did, but his partner didn't want social adeptness, she wanted a reassuring hug or wink, an outward display of togetherness!

We all love the great love stories, Tristan and Iseult, Romeo and Juliet, Guinevere and Lancelot. The most wonderful operas are about doomed love; 'Carmen,' 'Aida', and the films, the classic 'Brief encounter' 'Casablanca,' Gone with the Wind,'Ghost' 'Titanic' all have us reaching for our handkerchiefs.

But that level of overwhelming love happens all the time in real life.

From what I have learned through my seeing our past lives are many and group souls come back in family groups usually.

If there is a karmic contract between two souls to meet again who have loved each other for millennia that is going to create havoc in people's lives.

The reason we are so moved by these love stories of love that cannot be realized, is that it echoes within us, at the soul level, for we have known love in equally desperate intensity and we cry for ourselves, as well as the hero and heroine.

There is no justice in it. You could be a very devoted mother or father one minute and your life has altered in the next because the most overwhelming tsunami of emotion sweeps over you.

The trite phrase 'It was bigger than both of us' is actually true.

That intensity is born of countless lifetimes of being together, perhaps sometimes as lovers, or father and daughter or mother and son, but the soul remembers. It is instantaneous. Born in a moment. As if there had never been a moment's separation, for at the soul level, there hasn't.

The struggle to carry on with a marriage when the whole being is connected at the soul plane with the karmic .one who has returned is an enormous battle and is no one's fault.

That challenge was chosen before the group came back into incarnation and the roles they would play were already allocated.

That doesn't mean that the relationship has to be physical or that the partners decide to split. Where children are concerned different rules apply. Putting one's own happiness first at the expense of the happiness of children is an enormous dilemma.

It may be that it's a love of a different kind.

I have heard the same words of the identical experience a thousand times.

'We met at high school when I was twelve. I felt I had known him all my life.'

'We met when I was in my thirties, happily married with three lovely children. He had just moved in next door. When I looked at him, it was as if time stopped.'

'One day the door to my office opened. And I saw a man for the first time, my new boss but I knew him from that first second.'

'We never stopped talking. It was as if we had known each other all our lives but we'd only just met.'

'Even if we never married, I knew he was the love of my life and I could not live without him.'

'In that second our eyes met and my life would never be the same again.'

We were in a train and as I sat down and looked at this stranger I knew I had come home.'

Coming home seems to be the key concept here.

I know that it sounds like a romantic novel what's been written above.

It might be said that these are descriptions of falling in love at first sight.

But to my thinking it's remembered love from another time that immediately springs back into focus.

If this happens, the advanced soul may well experience déjà vu, where they are going between lifetimes simultaneously. The strain on their daily living becomes almost intolerable. If they tell their friends who haven't experienced anything like this, they think either they're delusional or it's instant attraction.

Morality is conditioned by where we live, our cultural bias and what society in that region determines to be right.

Religion doesn't dictate that women cover their bodies. Tribal customs do.

There is a great story, true about the British army in Borneo.

The indigenous people of Borneo Ibans and Penans, wore a woven skirt and no top so their breasts were bare. Their husbands were soldiers with the British army.

The British women found the presence of the bare breasted women an offence against their morals and went to the commander to demand that the native women covered themselves as was decent. So a large order was sent to Marks and Spencer for sensible, strong, white cotton bras.

They arrived. The commander sent for the man in the regiment who was known for his philandering ways, the Casanova of the battalion.

The women were lined up as the commander inspected them, with an ear cocked in the direction of his mentor, who muttered, as he looked at each in turn,

'34A, sir'

'36D, sir'

'32 AA, sir'

'38E! SIR'

Right down the line.

The commander holding out the appropriate garment.

Modesty prevailed and the Officers wives were content.

There is no easy way to deal with a karmic connection when it occurs in our life.

Nor should it be seen as an easy explanation for instant attraction which is to do with chemistry. A totally different thing and also challenging as well as healing, life sustaining and celebratory.

But the attraction is part of the soul level in the case of karmic love.

People use the terms soul mate and twin flame for they feel the other is exactly the match for them..

It becomes complicated when we realize there can be more than one soul mate in a lifetime.

Suppose we remember ourselves at twenty and who we were attracted to at that time.

Fast forward, to thirty, and we have changed and definitely the person we would choose then would be different from our choice aged twenty, for we've evolved.

Fast forward now to forty, fifty and so on.

I believe the first selection of mate is almost made for us by our reproductive selves finding the correct match for us to become parents. It is as if the universe knows the way for the advancement of the population..

This is at an unconscious level where we fall in love and marry or live together.

Over the years of people watching, I've noticed that if a mother has a small head, her husband will have a large one, and vice versa. I've never seen parents who have both got large heads or both small, in any culture. Maybe coincidence.

I do remember giving birth at home in Scotland which was unusual for the time, but I was adamant.

The midwife looked at my then husband who has a large head, mine is small, and said

'It'll be a slow birth, the child will have a big head'

True on both counts.

At thirty we know more about ourselves and so it progresses. Both partners seldom develop at the same rate.

This is not advocating changing partners every decade! No one accompanies us all the way through our lives but ourselves. Our parents predecease us, usually. We predecease our children, usually. Our siblings are older or younger than ourselves and our loves come into life at random times. The only constant, walking our path with us, is Nature itself, our first mother.

Karmic connections are powerful spurs to accelerate our growth, to give us choices. They can be for our well being and our destruction. They can have a short life energy or a lifelong influence.

In one of Soozi Holbeche's books, she describes running away from school in the States and going to her friend's house.

When she knocked at the door, her friend's uncle opened the door. As she looked at him, never having met him, she said,

'It's you again.'

And he said, simultaneously,

'You're back!'

And she ran away and they never met again. In that moment all was said.

We all dream and I think it's a good dream to hold to that we will have love which reaches every level of our being. Remembering that love has many faces, romantic, like a walz, passionate like a tango, gracious and dignified like a minuet and wild, a frenzy.

Actions have reactions. If not in this life time, in others

.Flowers don't grow in fields of blood.

Demanding that love is the ultimate goal no matter who gets hurt on the way is a hard burden to carry, once the flames have diminished a little.

I'm often given this picture while seeing for someone. Their partnership is shown in one hand like dry, desert sand, incapable of growing anything. The love they have for another is like soft, rich, earth capable of growing new life.

That is when it feels they may choose to let go of what is familiar but sterile, and choose life, at whatever risk!

It may be that the karmic love returns and the joy becomes tainted with jealousy and you realize it is destructive. One such person had been stabbed through the heart in ancient Egypt. The love had returned but the issue of jealousy had not been resolved even with the death in Egypt and he still was driven by that same need to possess totally. When she saw that she moved on.

If there is great love, unfulfilled, the lovers return. I see it as a game of hide and seek down the centuries

If there is great hate, the partners return to play it out to its conclusion.

Love and hate are opposite sides of the same coin.

And both will magnetise back in another lifetime.

To make sure this does not happen, if you have suffered greatly in this lifetime from someone, let go of hatred or love, feel neutrality.

If you die, feeling nothing, you will not come back together in another life time, for the dynamic between you is at an end.

Looking at the two most commonly described terms for all of the above Karmic connections may contain the following components

Power

A desire for dominance

Identity loss

Aggression

Disagreement

Vulnerability

Exhaustion

Stress

Isolation

Soul Mate connection

Supportive

Cooperatve

Equality

Sustaining

Open ended
Inspiring
Encouraging
Wholeness
Effortless
Home

I am quite sure you will have read soul mate and then realized it is a challenging karmic relationship which you have, which causes growth and life change. Often people think it's a soul mate and then realize a little way into the relationship that it's karmic.

The crimes of passion are usually karmic. The intensity of feeling is the dynamic which will take them into another round.

Important here to bring in will and intention. It is not Destiny which pushes us into intolerable situations and we have to submit. Never that!

We can use sublimation of one energy melded into another. We can use it as a dynamic for growth of our own talents. Repression won't work. That's when we get big psychological problems.

I believe seers can help enormously for they see the whole canvas, not only of this life time but where the roots are hidden and this knowledge helps release tension in the situation.

For the pull and tension are extremely hard to live with.

When two people are connected at the soul level, either karmically or as soul mates, there are cords of light attaching them to each other. Even if there are continents between them, the thoughts of one will be felt by the other. The dreams will be full of the other for we will have traveled in our sleep by astral projection, our ka, if you wish in Egyptian terms, slipping out of the head and going wherever we wish. Speaking to who ever we wish and who would pull us more than our beloved?

Love is the stuff of the Universe

Ways of helping you cope if you are in the situations outlined in the last chapter, are from my own experience.

Keep your feet firmly on the ground. If you are going through emotional trauma, your material security must not be affected especially if children are involved. You need to be strong and single minded for them.

In other words keep to your routine at work. Be punctual. Be efficient. Even if you have not slept, get up, shower and get on with the day.

Lying in bed, moping is never the answer.

If you say,

'I can't go on,' your problems are compounded by not being able to pay your bills for in these days of economic uncertainty, your employer will not be sympathetic to your emotional state.

Eat small amounts frequently. You won't have an appetite but don't let your health go down.

If you have a juicer, put carrot and spinach together and juice or blend, that is the perfect vegetable drink with all vitamins. Carrots have everything except iron which spinach has.

During the day raisins and almonds when you feel your energy is low. They have the perfect balance of fruits.

Exercise. Jogging, arerobics, gym sessions- exercise has a physiological effect on the body and emotions. Force yourself.

Alcohol is not an answer. It might temporarily dull the pain but it will intensify the emotions. Good to have a glass of red wine for health in the evenings though.

Someone I knew had one boy friend from age sixteen. They married when she was twenty one. She was an intelligent woman who felt very deeply. A languages teacher.

Her husband met someone at an office 'do' at a skittles night and aged twenty six he left her. She even made his sandwiches and a flask of coffee on the day he moved out.

Her coping mechanism was to drink a bottle of vodka every evening.

I couldn't believe it of this poised, well groomed young woman who never drank anything more than one white wine spritze if we went out.

As soon as she came out of the grief, her ordinary, sensible self took over.

It might well be that the pull of the cords of light is so unbearable that you wish to cut them and yourself free so you can have peace of mind again and enjoy ordinary things like lunches with friends, watching TV with your partner and appreciating Nature.

How to cut yourself free.

This is a magical operation (I've never studied magic)

Prepare yourself mentally. Be very sure you want to cut yourself free. It may be that to be strong enough, you have to think of the beloved's good which may require you not to be part of his life. So sacrifice of the self for another may be your springboard.

When you are alone and not likely to be disturbed by anyone for a couple of hours, visualize a cutting implement. It might be scissors, or a sharp knife. I used a diamond full of light.

See in your mind's eye where the cords are strongest. If you have a soul connection it will be the crown, the third eye centre between the eyebrows and the heart centre that will dominate.

The cord from the solar plexus is usually very thick.

If you communicate a lot by phoning or texting the throat centre of communication will be strongly corded.

One by one, with your intention and will focused, cut through the cords that bind you.

, from the third eye centre down, all the way through the seven chakras or wheels of light from whence the cords attach.

Immediately cauterize the ends which have been cut with fire.Visualising the fire, not actual fire!

You will feel spaced out and decidedly dizzy. Rest and drink some water.

Do this for at least a week or fortnight, for the cords will try to grow back between you, but weaker each time.

You may well lose weight and definitely the other will feel your energy which had been flowing between you. remove itself.

You will become stronger as you pull your colours back into your own aura.

He will become weaker for your energy has been withdrawn.

Some people seem to attract dramas into their lives and thrive on the emotional buzz.

Others are quietly intense.

When I lived many years ago in a small Scottish village there was a child I taught whose grandmother was bringing her up.

It was a beautiful small hamlet with no shops, rolling fields, a burn, rowan trees and in our garden a huge copper beech tree.

The little church was up the hill with the manse near it.

This grandmother was the essence of genteel Scottish womanhood. Her wavy white hair was always neat. Her fine woollen sweaters matched her good tweed skirts and her cairngorm brooch held her silk scarf in place.

One day at New Year she came to visit with her straw basket with a bottle of Harvey's Bristol Cream sherry for me and a bottle of whisky for my husband, for each of us to have glass to bring in the New Year. He never really surfaced till after midday on that day so I would measure his out for later as I got the black bun, shortbread and all other traditional foods for that celebration.

I said something about the new roof at the church, a pleasantry, and she changed in a flash from the sweet, gentle woman that I knew, into this passionate being..

'I dinna hae onything to do wi'the kirk. I dinna believe in God any mair since he took ma

Johnnie and him only sixteen and a fisherman. My love, ma Johnnie, and the sea took him. And I'll never step foot inside a church again.'

I was only in my twenties then and ventured,

'But you remarried, and have a daughter and a grand daughter. Doesn't that count for anything?

'Naethin' would make up for the loss of ma Johnnie '.

Fifty or more years must have gone by in her life since the drowning but it never left her.

We are, who we are, and are at the page we came in at, of our ongoing story.

My older son a journalist in Tokyo sent me a book called 'Singled Out' about the women who were left at the end of the First World War, only one in ten who would marry for there were virtually no men left.

How very strange that must have been for these women who would have grown up expecting their lives to follow in much the same pattern as their mothers. and how they would have sublimated their normal feelings and needs into being career women, carers for the elderly and dreaming of what might have been

Chapter 39

Nature

Having looked in some depth about breaking free from love entanglements which are karmic or soul mate connections which may impose too great a strain on the emotional nature, I'd like to look at the role Nature plays in our lives.

We know about diet and which foods are good for us. We know about the importance of keeping active for psychological, emotional and physical well being.

The vibrationary rate of the planet is increasing and understanding that we work with the environment, not imposing our will on it, is bringing us closer to Nature.

Germany has been in the forefront of herbal research and understanding since Hahnemann. Homeopathy is very important there and in every pharmacy there is a wide range of teas, tisanes, tinctures and creams from herbal sources. If someone is ill in Germany, in need of a restorative period of rest then after an analysis of the medical condition of the patient, a place is prescribed which suits the needs of the patient. It might be a high clear mountainous area for chest problems. For the heart a lake with trees around with no more than a gentle incline.. For bronchitis a pine forest for the inhalation of pine oil clears mucus from the chest. Others would need the bracing air of the sea to combat grief and depression.

In Ayurvedic practice juices are use for the relief of various ailments at the physical level which I will come to later on n this chapter.

In this, I want to look at the emotional imbalances which cause illness, eventually. Our.. weak spot will eventually succumb. It might be our head, migraines, our gut, tension and gastric ulcers, our heart for holding too much grief.

A method of preventing the manifestation of illness is the high vibrationary healing of flowers and herbs. If we treat the emotional state our health should benefit enormously.

Dr Edward Bach identified thirty eight remedies for emotional debilitating emotional states. Although a qualified doctor with a thriving practice he devoted himself to this study.

The remedies are taken as needed from a dropper with a blend of flower essences which a practitioner has intuited you need., Another method is for the patient to see what he is drawn to when he looks at the selection of healing bottles. Usually three essences together would be the norm but in extraordinary cases, up to seven may be given.

These essences are prepared in a solution of water but for longer lasting blends, a small measure of brandy is added to extend the life of the flower essence.

See if any of these resonate with you.

Centaury … people who allow themselves to become doormats, not standing up for them selves.

Elm…easily overwhelmed

Impatiens…. Impatient people

Beech…intolerance

Larch …lack of confidence

Cherry plum fear of losing

Crab apple ….obsessive compulsive in the way we view ourselves

Heather….all about 'me' jealousy

Baby blue eyes …father figure issues

Cerato ….self doubt

Gentian….easily discouraged

Gorse….hopelessness and despair

Hornbeam….procrastination, Monday morning feeling.

Wild oats …uncertainty

Vine….demanding

Agrimony….happy face on outside, crying inside

Alpine lily …for accepting the feminine side of themselves

White chestnut….scattered thoughts, inconsequential thoughts.

Walnut …protection from change

Goldenrod tea… for cat allergies

Sweet chestnut …..for terrible grief

Yellow star tulip …good for teachers and healers to restore energy

Zinnia …for living life with laughter and playfulness.

Corn….joy, living life fully

These are mixture of Bach remedies and North American flower remedies.

For example Baby blue eyes are from the desert of South America.

Since mostly we go for help when we're down. in the main it's mostly the negative aspects that have been given for you to identify with.

Holly positively...feeling love and sharing with others. In its negative aspect, feeling cut off from love, envy, anger

So if we are smart, we identify a persistent emotional imbalance and rectify it, so that the imbalance does not bring on illness further down the line.

I have the feeling too that proximity to the flower itself in the garden and knowing its healing qualities would enhance your enjoyment of the garden and your health at the same time, for you would be interacting with the soul essence of the flower, not merely admiring it!

When I am in orchid centres while admiring the beauty of the bloom, I always feel as if they are half way between flowers and animals. Maybe because I saw so many pitcher plants in the jungle of Borneo in the process of digesting flying insects!

The flower remedies are for working at a high vibration to stop conditions arising which cause bad health.

They shouldn't be stored anywhere near electricity or batteries.

Studying Ayurveda was to help people with ailments through diet and massage and I believe these two fields are complementary.. Agrimony is used in flower essences and it is used as a tea for prevention of cancer in Ayurvedic healing. Two cups of tea a day.

.The time spent working with people, preparing clay and nutmeg for joint pain was truly fascinating. People from all walks of life with one thing in common. They all had a real respect for the healer's knowledge and were ready to change their lives and habits to maximize their health prospects.

He treated diet as essential for arthritic conditions. He advocated natural food preferably raw salads or steamed foods. We learned how to make pepper soup for bad colds and reducing fever.

One day a doctor from the nearby hospital came for he had a soft non malignant cyst on his Adam's apple. It had been x-rayed and a biopsy had been done to make sure that it was benign.

However surgery was something he wanted to avoid and he turned to the healer. I was to attend to him, following instructions of course.

He was to come daily for at least two weeks, so it was a fair commitment of time for this doctor to drive from the hospital to the other side of town.

He was told to sit in a chair. I was told to get a stone which was used for rubbing down the clay to make a fine solution, but this time, I was to take an elephant's molar and with water, rub hard till I got a white paste.

I did this. It took a long time to get the consistency. I then applied the white paste to the soft mass over the Adam's apple.

I caught the eye of the doctor and truly it was hard not to laugh at his expression. We both had total faith in this dedicated healer who was also a lecturer in physics at a local college..

I don't think either of us really believed this remedy would work, but day after day, the swelling grew less. Finally there was nothing left but the Adam's apple.

We both asked why this should have the power to heal and the reply was,

'It is only the molar that heals and the elephant eats all kinds of leaves and herbs. It is believed that that is the reason for the enormous healing of the molar.'

I tried in vain by writing to museums for a molar but all refused. It wasn't for me but a good Kashmiri man who had one eye disfigured by a huge cyst from birth on his upper eyelid. No money for cosmetic surgery in that part of the world

Here are some of the juices which you can take when you identify an ailment you have.

Apple....blood purifier and good for morning sickness.

Apricot....cleanser, good for asthma and diarrhea

Avocado..... good for ulcers, insomnia and impotence

Bananas ....good for the heart

Blackberries ....a nerve tonic and catarrh

Cherries ...good for arthritis

Dates .... For anaemia and sleeplessness

Figs..... for heart and exhaustion

Gooseberry......for eye problems

Grapes....for kidney and liver

Grapefruit...... for gallstone and pregnant women

Guava...... for diabetes

Lemon.....solves uric acid in the body and good for headaches

Olive ....prevents cholesterol forming

Oranges…good for nervous system

Peel is a natural antihistamine

Peach for indigestion

Pear….for kidney stones

Pomegranate …..good for the heart

Pineapple ….to cure nicotine poisoning

Plum….for bleeding gums

Prune…calms the mind

Raisins….for low blood pressure

Star fruit….for kidney and bladder problems

Strawberry….. for sore throats

Watermelon….diuretic

Knowing these simple things about fruit can improve our quality of life and health.

Anti aging, coconut

The mineral kingdom also gives us healing. Think about taking your daily minerals, potassium, magnesium, zinc and so on.

If I go into a room, I'll always recognize the signature of the crystalline vibration. It might be a geode tucked away behind a vase or a crystal sitting on a window ledge, but it's emanating.

I was doing crystal healing in Shanghai and I had placed my own healing crystals on the patient. I was suddenly aware that not only were my crystals working, but so were all the others in the room, working.

The quartz crystals on the coffee table, the amethyst on he window ledge. The citrine near the plants, all actively sending out to the patient.

I found this amazing. At a high vibrationary frequency they were all in unison.

When I see crystals which haven't been dusted, I feel sad, for the vitality is diminished.

Simply dusting with a feather duster seems to get the ions moving and it's almost like seeing them dance in a shower! They become so alive.

Every mineral has its own healing property.

Rutilated quartz will help steady the ambitions and help in procuring a new job. It keeps one focused.

Citrine is for cheerfulness and abundance in all ways.

Rose quartz is for healing the heart of sadness and loneliness.

Garnet is strengthening the body and mind.

Agates ground us and make us feel safe.

Silver is antibiotic.

Gold is an antidepressant. If you put a gold ring or earring into a glass of water, leave it overnight and, after removing, drink the water, it will lift your spirits in much the same way as St John's Wort.

Go into a gem shop and just see what calls you. The mineral will choose you, not the other way round.

To cross check buy a little book which gives the significance of stones and you will find that exactly what your emotional or physical state was at the time, the stone is an absolute match.

Tektites or shooting stars that fall to earth have a fascination for me and I have found so many and given them to family and friends. They look like black orange peel, pitted with striations for they come through the earth's atmosphere and are shaped by it. They are in round or pear shapes and they act as a fishing net, bringing things to you. They cost next to nothing but they are powerful minerals to carry. I personally prefer them to Moldavite which is a combination of the earth and the sky energy impacting on collision.

Wear them or keep them on your desk or under your pillow. Make them part of your life as life enhancing helpers. They do change according to our moods. I had a turquoise ring and it was in a drawer for ages. One day I put it on and went to school. My colleague who didn't know anything about minerals remarked after three days,

';You know I've been watching that stone. Every day the colour is getting stronger.'

It was true. From lying, neglected it was sparklingly bright. Opals react in the same way.

Colour is a healing agent at every level. Psychologically it gives us a boost when we're down.

Wearing black says' Back off ...I need space!'

Yellow stimulates, so should never be used to decorate a child's bedroom. All right if he has a room for studying in, then it keeps the brain active.

A soft pastel will induce sleep.

Pink is used in high security prisons with violent criminals. There is an immediate improvement in behaviour in this coloured environment.

Red is needed to be absorbed into the body when we are weak. We can do this simply by eating red fruits and vegetables, or drinking solarised water from a red glass.

It is not a good colour for decorating a room. It can cause arguments.

Blue is soothing and calming.

Green is good for the heart but not if there are any tumours, benign or otherwise,

It makes them grow.

Violet causes them to shrink.

Orange as an oil or colour makes us feel upbeat and optimistic.

Chapter 40

conclusion

This is the life's work to date of one seer. My work began, I think, from a young age for the seeing was always there. In the family group I believe I protected the others as much as I could from around age four..

A characteristic of this life time is definitely hard work, in raising four children, having an academic career, changing horses in mid stream as it were., being always in service in some way. Being responsible for the health of the students and teachers in a large school where I studied every winter for my St John's ambulance award. A union leader trying to safeguard the good practices in schools to improve education. Involved in the welfare of teachers in Brunei while teaching, studying healing and using my higher gifts.

My way was to be born the seer and then bring healing forward.

I first studied yoga and was a yoga teacher, Hatha. Later in Bali I studied Raja yoga.

The next discipline was studying colour and crystal healing and becoming a practitioner.

Then came the years of studying Ayurveda.

From then I studied Advanced crystal healing, Reiki to Master Level, Indian head massage, Neuro Linguistic Programming and finally Flower Essence Healing.

The learning process never ends. Even at the end of our lives, we'll only have our toes in the water!

The seer is in everything I do, whether it is teaching, healing, giving a demonstration to a large or small group, writing, conference calls, meditation groups, making CD's, doing encaustic wax art, creating jewelry from appropriate minerals, whatever.

I go when the call comes for I don't advertise anywhere in the world. All invitations have come through word of mouth

.I have handed over my life in a sense to the Universe, trusting that by submitting to the highest good, all will be well.

These two books have emerged from the inner dictates of what I was to do on my spiritual path.

I got heartily sick of fellow seers saying,

'Your guides are saying your book is very overdue!'

I felt really indignant. Wasn't I going to far and distant places? Wasn't I working hard and always the reply.

'Excuses!'

So last November and December, 2008, I wrote solidly for two months from nine am to

6pm every day.

This month of August 2009, in three weeks I have written this, the sister book to the first, about the skills, about being a seer, about ways that you, may help advance your life by something that has been written here which may resonate with you.

We co create our. reality. The magic is all around us in Nature. We just have to open our eyes to see. And feel the joy and laughter.'

I was told I had books to write. This was my mission.(The third,' A Seer's Song' was finished 2nd September 2011)

Done!

I wish you light in your mists.

Kallepeia

Paphos

Cyprus

26th August 2020

Printed in the United States
By Bookmasters